Only in America:

Our sayings, Expressions, and Pearls of Wisdom

Jacqueline K. "Jackie" Hughes

Visit Heaven Press—Sumter, SC
Paperback ISBN: 979-8-218-49032-4
eBook ISBN: 979-8-3304-1837-4
Library of Congress Control Number: 2024916765
Title: *Only in America: Our sayings, expressions, and Pearls of Wisdom*
Author: Jacqueline K. "Jackie" Hughes
Digital distribution | 2024
Paperback | 2024

Dedication

I want to thank everyone who helped in some way to bring this book to be published. I especially want to thank my cousin and good friend, Nancy Weatherly Jordan and my son Theodore "Teddy" Hughes, who helped with the computer and contributions. Without their help this wouldn't have happened.

Also, my good friend, Stephanie Gibbons, who always helps me with the computer. And of course, Erica with New Book Authors.

Table of Contents

Introduction

I am writing this book about saying, because I don't think that younger people are aware of them in the United States today. Back in about 2012 I was a substitute teacher and was in a math class. It was a 4th grade class and they were doing the math the teacher had assigned. One of the students wanted me help the class with a problem. I ask if one of the students would like to show the class how to work the problem. One of the students volunteered. When he finished, I asked the class if they wanted to know how to do it in an easier way.

They told me they had to do it the way they were taught. I said OK "but there is more than one way to skin a cat." One of the girls starting crying. I asked her why she was crying and she said that I said I was going to skin a cat. I explained that I did not say what she was thinking that I said. I asked her to go home and ask her grandmother what I meant. I could have explained it to her but I really didn't think that she was capable of knowing what I was saying. I have no idea that she went home and asked her grandmother what it meant.

I have thought a lot about that situation since it happened. I just keep wondering how many everyday sayings are understood or misunderstood by those that are young.

I have been collecting saying since then. I have now put them on paper. I have broken them down by subject. I will not try to explain them because we all have to figure out what they mean as that is part of growing up. We say them many times a day without even thinking about it.

There is no way I could ever think up all the saying because they are as numerous as the stars in the sky or the sand on the sea shores. Just kidding. I have no idea how many there could have been since the start of time to this very day.

Let's get going. Enjoy yourself.

Addictions of all kinds

Are you being judgmental? Judging another child of God or are you using good judgment? Knowing when someone else is dangerous for you to be with.

As for me and my house, we will serve the Lord. (Joshua 24:15)

Be careful what you ask for, you just might get it. Then what?

Before passing judgement on anyone, walk in his shoes for a couple of weeks.

Being dry is not being sober!

Do you prefer to be Right or Happy?

Easy does it.

Evil prevails- when good people do nothing.

FACE is to be aware, ERASE is to forgive and REPLACE is to change.

Failure is not final! It may be a detour, but is doesn't have to be a dead end.

FEAR knocked on the door, FAITH opened it to find no one there.

First things first!

4 Paradoxes - 1. die to live, 2. surrender to win, 3. be sick to get well, and 4. give it away to keep it!

God helps us when we can't help ourselves.

God loves each one of us as if there were only one of us. (Saint Augustine)

H-A-L-T-S (don't get to Hungry, Angry, Lonely, Tired or Stressed.)

Happy, joyous and free, is what I want to be!

Help me to remember God, that nothing is going to happen today, that YOU and I can't handle together.

Honesty is Truth and the Truth shall set me free!

I am what I am and that's all that I am.

I don't care how much you know, until I know how much you care.

I judge myself by my intentions, but the world judges me by my actions.

I pray - not to change God's mind, but to ask God to change mine.

I was angry with a foe, I told him not, it did grow. I was angry with a friend, I told him so, it did end.

I was in such Denial, that I didn't even know, what I didn't even know.

I would rather be here by mistake, then be out there by mistake.

If I have to explain, you wouldn't understand.

If I spend all my time looking for Your faults, then I don't have the time to look for My own.

If it is to be it is up to me! (Ten 2 letter words)

If you Pray, don't worry! If you Worry, don't pray!

If you understand or you don't, if you believe or if you doubt, there's a universal justice. And the eyes of truth are always watching you!

If you want a compliment, give one. You have to give to receive.

If you want to understand me, identifying is just the key. Comparing for you will see, will cause it not to be.

If your thinking is stinking, please be kind and change your mind.

I'm a victim of my own thoughts and actions. What I think and do always comes back to me.

It isn't you drinking that's stinking...It's your thinking!

Keep the Faith.

Let go and let God!

Live and let live.

Live well, Love much and Laugh often.

Miracles happen to those who believe in them.

Most people are about as happy as they make up their minds to be.

My way may not be the right way, since it doesn't even work for me.

My purpose here on Earth is that I bear witness unto the Truth.

Never give up. It's always darkest before dawn.

Never give up. The tide always turns at its lowest point.

No God - No Peace. Know God - Know Peace!

One day at a time, One moment at a time.

One step at a time.

Poor Me, Poor Me, Pour Me, another drink.

P - U - S - H - Pray Until Something Happens

Pray and Meditation. Talking to God-Listening for God's answer.

Rule #1 - Don't sweat the Small Stuff! Rule #2 - It's all Small Stuff!

Say what you mean. Mean what you say.

Selfishness- Self-centeredness! That, we think, is the root of all our troubles. So, our troubles, we think are of our own making.

Serenity is directly proportional to my level of acceptance and inversely proportional to my expectations.

Take what you want and leave the rest. It's all up to You.

Teach Only Love, for that is what you are. (A Course in Miracles)

The ability to choose, YOUR response- is being "Response-able!

The 7 Deadly sins. Pride, Greed, Lust, Anger, Gluttony Envy, Sloth

The Disease of Alcoholism is Threefold, 1. The Problem - is Emotional, 2. The Symptom - is Physical, 3. The Solution - is Spiritual.

The Door swings both ways, You can GO OUT and You can COME BACK IN.

The first step in solving a problem is the admit to the problem.

The Key to failure is trying to please everybody.

The most fundamental Law is the Law of Cause and Effect. Cause - thoughts and actions, Effect - the result of those thoughts and actions.

The Rules apply to everyone! and YOU don't get to be an exception!

The way You see a PROBLEM - IS THE PROBLEM! Remember - You can change your mind!

There is CASH in CHAOS! Are you part of the PROBLEM or part of the ANSWER?

Things do not change; We change.

There but for the Grace of God go I.

We are on a journey without distance to a goal that has never changed. (A Course in Miracles)

Whether you believe you can or believe you can't, either way you're right. (Henry Ford)

What you are is God's gift to you; what you become is your gift to God.

What your mind can conceive, you can achieve!

When I focus on the problem, the problem increases. When I focus on the answer the answer increases.

When the gates are down and the signals are flashing, and the whistle is screaming in vain, if you stay on the tracks ignoring the facts then don't blame the wreck on the train.

When one door closes, another opens. (by Alexander Graham Bell)

When the Student is ready, the Teacher will appear. We are all Teachers to each other.

With God all things are possible. (Matthew 19:26)

Regular Sayings

A

A bad beginning often makes a good ending.
A bad penny always returns.
A barking dog never bites.
A big fish tale.
A big wheel.
A bushel and a peck and a hug around your neck.
A busy bee.
A chain is only as strong as its weakest link.
A chip off the old block.
A cool cat.
A diamond is a girl's best friend.
A dog is man's best friend.
A drowning man will grasp at a straw.
A few good men.
A fool and his money are soon parted.
A friend in need is a friend in deed.
A friend is one who tells you of your faults and helps you to mend them.
A good laugh is the best of medicine.
A good name is rather to be chosen than great riches.
A guilty conscience needs no accuser.
A hop, skip, and a jump.
A kick in the pants.
A laugh a minute.
A lie can go around the world before truth has time to put on its boots.
A little help is worth a great deal of pity.
A little knowledge is a dangerous thing.
A little of this and a little of that.
A lot of shenanigans.

A lot of water has gone under the bridge since we last met.
A man convinced against his will is of the same opinion still.
A man is known by the company he keeps.
A miss is as good as a mile.
A new broom sweeps clean.
A nickel isn't worth a dime anymore.
A one-track mind.
A peeping Tom.
A penny for your thoughts.
A penny saved is a penny earned.
A picture is worth a thousand words.
A piece of money.
A poor excuse is better than none.
A prayer is simply a wish turned heavenward.
A promise is a promise.
A rag, a bone, and a hank of hair.
A rattle-brain.
A real kick in the head.
A red-hot mamma.
A regular fuss-budget.
A regular jumping Jack.
A regular rattle trap.
A rising tide lifts all boats.
A rolling stone gathers no moss.
A safe and sane July Fourth.
A sailor has a girl in every port.
A school girl crush.
A sight for sore eyes.
A stitch is time saves nine.
A straight line is the shortest distance between two points.
A strong back and a weak mind.
A thing-a-bob.
A thing-a-ma-jig.
A tree is known by its fruit.
A watched pot never boils.
A whirl-a-ma-gig.
A wise man questions himself, a fool, and others.
A woman has a right to change her mind.
Able to sit up and take nourishment.

About the only difference between a gold stripe and a yellow stripe
is - where you find it.
Abracadabra
Absence makes the heart grow fonder.
Accidents will happen in the best of families.
According to Hoyle.
Act your age.
Action speaks louder than words.
Afraid of your own shadow.
After all, boys will be boys.
Age is just a state of mind.
Age of Deception.
Ain't ain't in the dictionary.
Ain't he a card?
Ain't that the truth?
All ashore that's going ashore.
All bad is compensated by good.
All day long.
All dressed up and no place to go.
All for one and one for all.
All good things come to those who wait.
All good things must come to an end.
All is fair in love and war.
All men are created equal.
All right boys, come and get it.
All right, cough it up.
All right, prove it.
All roads lead to Rome.
All shook up.
All that glitters is not gold.
All the days of our lives.
All this have and have nots, in and outs.
All up in arms about it.
All washed up.
All work and no play makes Jack a dull boy.
All's well that ends well.
Alpha and Omega
Alright, you asked for it.
Always behind like a cow's tail.
Always chewing the rag.

Always Faithful. Semper Fi Semper Fidel's
Always kicking.
Always mind the golden rule, and learn your lessons well at school.
Always shooting off your mouth.
Always sticking their nose in other people's business.
America! the land of the free.
An apple a day keeps the doctor away.
An eye for an eye and a tooth for a tooth.
An elephant never forgets.
An idle brain is the devil's workshop.
An inward sorrow is a consuming fire.
An ounce of prevention is worth a pound of cure.
And the wind blew through his whiskers.
And they lived happily ever after.
Another day, another dollar.
Anticipation is greater than realization.
Any old port in a storm.
Any old port in time of storm.
Anything new?
Apple pie without cheese is like a hug without a squeeze.
Apples of gold in pictures of silver.
April fool.
Are we there yet?
Are you game to do it?
As correct as pretzels with beer.
As empty as a sieve.
As far as I know.
As hard to find as a needle in a haystack.
As honest as the day is long.
As if I cared.
As stingy as a Scotchman.
As the crow flies.
As the tree falls, so shall it lie.
As the twig is bent so grows the tree.
As the twig is bent so the tree is inclined.
As welcome as the flowers in May.
As wrinkled as a prune.
As you sow so ye shall reap.
Ask me no questions and I'll tell you no lies.

Ask not what your country can do for you, ask what you can do for
your country.
Ass backwards.
At least I have a toe-hold.
At the crack of dawn.
At the tail end.
Auf Wiedersehn.
Aw, go chase yourself.

B

Baby face.
Back in the good old days.
Back to the salt mines.
Bald as an eagle.
Bankers hours.
Barging in like a bull in a china shop.
Basement Dwellers.
Basket of deplorables.
Batting his eyes like a toad in a hailstorm.
Be careful what you wish for!
Be careful who you talk about, they might be a cousin.
Be gone.
Be my baby.
Be my gal.
Be my guy.
Be jabers.
Be my valentine.
Be not wise in your own conceit.
Be of good cheer!
Be prepared.
Be quiet as a mouse.
Be safe, be smart, be kind.
Be sure your sins will find you out.
Be wise!
Beat it.
Beauty is as beauty does.
Beauty is in the eye of the beholder.
Beauty is only skin deep.
Because of need discoveries are born.
Beef steak that is rare cuts easy, but, Beef steak that cuts easy is rare.
Beggars cannot be choosers.
Behind closed door.
Behind the 8 ball.
Behind the times.
Believe it or not.
Better late than never.

Better put your thinking cap on.
Better safe than sorry.
Better to light one candle than to sit in darkness.
Better wash behind your ears.
Better watch out or your name will be mud.
Between the Devil and the deep blue sea.
Big as a barn.
Big as an elephant.
Birds of a feather flock together.
Bitter as gall.
Blabber mouth.
Blacker than a chaw of tobacco.
Black as a bear or coal.
Black as ink.
Bless you.
Bless your heart.
Bless your pea-pickin' heart.
Blessed be nothing.
Blind as a bat.
Blood is thicker than water.
Blow 'em down.
Blow the man down.
Blowing out someone else's candle does not make yours shine any brighter.
BOGO (Buy one get one free).
BOLO (Be on the lookout for __________)
Bon voyage.
Bone up on it.
Boondoggling.
Boop, boop, e doo.
Boot 'em out.
Brave as a lion.
Bread and butter.
Bread is the staff of life.
Break the news.
Breaking the ice.
Breaking the record.
Bright as a dollar.
Bright-eyes and bushy-tailed.
Bring 'em back dead or alive.

Bring it.
Bring it on.
Bring it on home.
Bring out the white elephant.
Bringing home the bacon.
Brown as a berry.
Brush your hair 100 times a day.
Brush your teeth.
Buck up.
Bumble bee bumble bee, came from the farm, and stung little Johnny right under the arm.
Burned to a crisp.
Burning bridges at both ends.
Burning the candle at both ends.
Burning your bridges behind you.
Busier than a cat on a tin roof.
Busy as a beaver.
Busy as a bee.
Butter fingers.
Button your lip.
By cracky!
By George.
By gosh, by golly.
By guess and by golly.
By hook or by crook.
By Joe!
By Jove.
By the great horn spoon.
By the skin of your teeth.

C

Call a spade a spade.
Call me!
Call me back!
Can you hear me now?
Can you imagine that?
Can you stop that?
Can you top that?
Can't never did anything.
Can't you get that through your thick skull.
Care for some hot milk?
Catch a falling star and put it in your pocket.
Catch as catch can.
Caught in his own trap.
Caught in the act.
Caught with you hand in the cookie jar.
Charity cover a multitude of sins.
Check and double check.
Cheerio.
Cheese it.
Chewing the rag.
Chickens come home to roost.
Children should be seen and not heard.
Circumstances alter cases.
Clear as a crystal.
Clear as a whistle.
Clear out of here.
Clockwise - Righty Tighty (see "counter clockwise")
Close your peepers.
Clothed and in his right mind.
Cold as an iceberg.
Cold as an icicle.
Colder than ice.
Come and get it.
Come and take it.
Come down off your high horse.
Come down to earth awhile.

Come fly with me.
Come now, fess up.
Come off your high horse.
Come on, dig in.
Come out, come out, wherever you are.
Come over to dinner.
Consider the source.
Cool as a cucumber.
Cool as an ocean breeze.
Couldn't hold a candle to it.
Count me out.
Counter-clockwise - Lefty Loosey (see "clockwise")
Counting sheep to go to sleep.
Cowabunga.
Crazy as a bedbug.
Crazy as a loon.
Crazy man crazy.
Crime does not pay.
Crime doesn't pay.
Crooked as a corkscrew.
Cross as a bear.
Cross my heart.
Cross my heart and hope to die.
Curiosity killed the cat but satisfaction brought it back.
Cut it out.
Cute as a bugs ear.
Cutting a rug.

D

Dark as a dungeon.
Darn your hide.
Daylight saving time.
Dead as a door nail.
Dead men tell no tales.
Deader than a door nail.
Deaf as an adder.
Did she marry for love or money?
Did you blow your stack?
Did you ever hear the likes of it?
Did you get the mazuma?
Didn't I tell you?
Dirty as a pig.
Discretion is the better part of valor.
*Distracted driving.
Ditto.
Do I have to put it in writing?
Do it now.
Do it, pronto.
Do it yourself.
Do jigger.
Do unto other as you would have them do unto you.
Do what you must today for tomorrow may never come.
Do what you want.
Do you dig it?
Do you do windows?
Do you have skin in the game?
Do you know your oats?
Do you love me?
Do you really care?
Do you swear to tell the truth, the whole truth and nothing but the truth, so help me God?
Do your stuff.
Doctors orders.
Dodging the issue.
Does it send you?
Dog-gone-it.

Dog gone it, anyway.
Doing her daily dozen.
Doing what comes naturally.
Dom de born unt nicht zu gelernt. (German)
Done to a fare ye well.
Don't act so high and mighty.
Don't back down.
Don't be a litter bug.
Don't be a sucker.
Don't be an ass!
Don't be so uppity.
Don't believe your lying eyes.
Don't bite the hand that feeds you.
Don't blow your stack.
Don't blow your top.
Don't call me back!
Don't care whether school keeps or not.
Don't change horses in the middle of the stream.
Don't count your chickens before they are hatched.
Don't cross the bridge before you get to it.
Don't cross the line.
Don't cry over spilled milk.
Don't cut off your nose to spite your face.
Don't do anything I wouldn't do.
Don't fence me in.
Don't fire until you can see the whites of their eyes.
Don't fire until you have a target.
Don't flip your lid.
Don't fly off the handle.
Don't give up the ship.
Don't go beating around the bush.
Don't go bellyaching around.
Don't go into a tall spin.
Don't go shootin' all the dogs cause one of them's got fleas.
Don't gum up the works.
Don't have a fit.
Don't hide your light under a bushel.
Don't hold your breath until it happens.
Don't judge a man until you walk 24 hours in his shoes.
Don't jump to conclusions.

Don't kick a gift horse in the mouth.
Don't kill the goose that lays the golden egg.
Don't knock it until you've tried it.
Don't let it dampen your spirits.
Don't let the bedbugs bite.
Don't let the cat out of the bag.
Don't look a gift horse in the mouth.
Don't look for trouble where there isn't any because if you don't find it, you'll make it.
Don't louse it up.
Don't make a fool of yourself.
Don't make baby clothes until the wedding.
Don't pass the buck.
Don't put all of your eggs in one basket.
Don't put all your bees in one hive.
Don't put off until tomorrow what you can do today.
Don't put the cart before the horse.
Don't put your foot in it.
Don't rock the boat!
Don't spill the beans.
Don't spit on the sidewalk.
Don't stand on ceremony.
Don't stand there like a bump on a log.
Don't stick your neck out.
Don't stick your nose into other people's business.
Don't! Stop! Don't! Stop! Don't stop.
Don't take any wooden nickels.
Don't take chances.
Don't take life too seriously for you're not going to get out of it alive.
Don't throw a fit.
Don't throw good money after bad.
Don't try to change horses in the middle of the stream.
Don't upset the apple cart.
Don't wait til the last minute.
Don't wear your heart on your sleeve!
Don't worry, be happy.
Don't you believe it.
Drill, baby, drill!
Driven from pillar to post.

Drop dead.
Drop me a line.
Dry as powder.

E

E pluribus unum. (One of many)

Early to bed and early to rise, makes a man healthy, wealthy and wise.

Earn your own bread and butter.

East is east and west is west and never the twain shall meet.

Easy does it.

Easy peasy.

Eat hair of the dog.

Eating high on the hog.

Eating his own words.

Eating peanuts by the peck.

Eaves droppers never hear any good of themselves.

Egghead.

Equal justice for all.

Even a fish wouldn't get into trouble if he kept his mouth shut.

Even Steven.

Even the Devil can cite scripture for his purpose.

Every cloud has a silver lining.

Every dog has his day.

Every little bit helps.

Every man for himself.

Everybody loves a lover.

Everyone is innocent until proven guilty.

Everyone to their own notion.

Everything is topsy turvy.

Everything stops for tea.

Evil to him who evil thinks.

Experience is the best teacher.

Eyes to see and ears to hear.

F

Face the music.
Faint heart never won fair lady.
Fair to middling.
Familiarity breeds contempt.
Fancy that.
Fandangle
Fat as a pig.
Father, I can not tell a lie, I cut the tree. George Washington
Feather brain.
Feed the kitty.
Feeling your oats.
Fiddle dee dee.
Fight fire with fire.
Fight if you must.
Figures don't lie.
Find a left-handed monkey wrench.
Finders keepers, losers weepers.
Fine or superfine?
Finer than frog's hair.
First come, first served.
First love is the best.
Fishing for favor.
Fit as a fiddle.
Fit as a fiddle and ready for love.
Flat as a pancake.
Flip a coin.
Flip the bird.
Flirting with danger.
For auld lang syne.
For crying out loud.
For every action there is an equal and opposite reaction. Newton's third law
For goodness sake.
For heaven's sake.
For land's sake.
For Pete's sake.
For Pete's sake, where have you been keeping yourself?

For sure.
For the love of God.
For the love of money.
For weal or woe.
Four on the sidewalk's not allowed.
Fraidy cat.
Free and clear.
Freedom isn't free.
Fresh as a daisy.
Friendly as a puppy.
Frisky as a lamb.
From out in the sticks.
From the frying pan into the fire.
Funny as a crutch.
Fuzzy as a caterpillar.

G

Gathering up the loose ends.
Gay as a lark.
Gee whillikers.
Generation X.
Get a little backbone.
Get a wiggle on.
Get going.
Get going while the going's good.
Get happy.
Get hep to it.
Get him dead or alive.
Get it down in black and white.
Get on board.
Get on the ball.
Get on the band wagon.
Get rich or die trying.
Get right with God.
Get set.
Get, while the getting's good.
Get your COVID shot and boosters.
Getting a face lift.
Getting something for nothing.
Getting their heads together.
Giddy.
Giddy up.
Gimme, gimme.
Git, while the gittings good.
Give credit where credit is due.
Give 'em a run for their money.
Give 'em an inch and they'll take an ell.
Give 'em the once over.
Give him a break.
Give him a run for his money.
Give him an inch and he'll take a mile.
Give him rope enough and he'll hang himself.
Give him the Indian sign.
Give him the works.

Give him what he's due.
Give me a ring.
Give me liberty or give me death.
Give me your best.
Give someone the bird.
Give the calf more rope.
Give the devil his due.
Give the world a smile.
Give us the straight scoop.
Giving the cold shoulder.
Glad to have you aboard.
Go chase yourself.
Go fly a kite.
Go grab a hat.
Go jump in a lake.
Go play your fiddle.
Go soak your head.
Go to blazes.
Go to Goggle.
Go to the devil.
Go west young man, go west.
Go woke, Go broke.
GOAT - Greatest of all time.
God be with you, until we meet again.
God Bless America!
God Bless the USA!
God helps those who help themselves.
God loves you!
Going in one door and coming out another brings company.
Going like a blue streak.
Going Scot free.
Gold and silver are less precious than beauty and love.
Gold is where you find it.
Gone but not forgotten.
Gone with the wind.
Good as gold.
Good Bye.
Good fences make good neighbors.
Good heavens.
Good luck, if a penny is found heads up.

Good morning, how are you?
Good night nurse.
Good old Irish spuds.
Goodbye.
Grass doesn't grow on a busy street.
Gray as a rat.
Great balls of fire.
Great Caesar!
Great day in the morning.
Great guns and little fishes.
Great minds run in the same channel.
Great oaks from little acorns grow.
Great Scott.
Grievous words stir up anger.
Grin and bear it.

H

Had turkey and all the trimmings.
Half a loaf is better than none.
Half a pie is better than no pie at all.
Handy Andy.
Hands off.
Hands up.
Handsome is as handsome does.
Hanky-panky.
Happy as a lark.
Happy birthday to you.
Happy Easter!
Happy 4th of July.
Happy landings.
Happy New Year!
Happy trails to you, until we meet again.
Hard as a rock.
Hard to please.
Hard work never killed anyone.
Harder than a door knob.
Haste makes mistakes.
Haste makes waste.
Hats off to you.
Haul him off to the hoosegow.
Have a great day.
Have you gone off your rocker?
Haven't seen you since the cows came home.
Having a whale of a good time.
Hay foot, straw foot, hay foot, straw foot.
He beat him to the draw.
He beats his fists against the posts and still insists he sees the ghosts.
He blew his top.
He can whistle for his money.
He can't hit the broad side of a barn.
He can't run for sour apples.
He cleaned everything out, lock, stock, and barrel.
He cleaned me out.
He could run like greased lightning.

He deserves a kick in the pants.
He did a 180 degrees.
He drinks like a fish.
He eats like a horse.
He fell for it.
He fell for it, hook, line and sinker.
He flew off the handle.
He gave her a moth eaten line.
He gave him a run for his money.
He got an eyeful.
He got it in the neck.
He got off on the wrong foot.
He had a cool million.
He had a strange look on his face.
He had a strangle hold.
He has a face that only a mother could love.
He has a 50-50 chance.
He has a frog in his throat.
He has a high water mark.
He has a wheel loose somewhere.
He has a yellow streak.
He has an axe to grind.
He has cold feet.
He has the dough.
He has the evil eye.
He has the patience of Job.
He has the right shoe on the wrong foot.
He has the slick manners and a glib tongue.
He has too many irons in the fire.
He hasn't got a leg to stand on.
He hasn't got all of his marbles.
He hit him in the solar plexus.
He hit the jackpot.
He hit the nail on the head.
He invoked his right to remain silent.
He is in it to win it.
He is rubbing me the wrong way.
He is sure set in his ways.
He jumped down my throat!
He kicked the bucket.

He killed two birds with one stone.
He knows what I am thinking.
He knows which side his bread is buttered on.
He laid all his cards out on the table.
He landed in the cooler.
He let the cat out of the bag.
He lies like a rug.
He lived hand to mouth.
He locks the barn after the house is stolen.
He loves me, he loves me not.
He made a big strike.
He made a monkey of himself.
He must have a cast iron stomach.
He needs a kick in the pants.
He needs his head examined.
He ought to have his head examined.
He popped the question.
He put me through hell and high water.
He put me through the wringer.
He read the riot act.
He really leaned over backwards.
He remained in their crosshairs.
He says one thing to your face, and another behind your back.
He sold them down the river.
He struck the nail on the head.
He swallowed it, hook, line, and sinker.
He swears like a mule skinner.
He that digs a pit shall fall therein.
He that lies down with dogs will wake up with fleas.
He thinks he is a big shot.
He took French leave.
He treats her like a dog.
He was born with a silver spoon in his mouth.
He was hog-tied.
He was hood-winked.
He was off base a country mile.
He was scared out of his wits.
He was the town crier.
He went berserk.
He will argue the leg off the pot.

He who crows last crows loudest.
He who fights and runs away, May live to run another day.
He who has himself for a doctor has a fool for a patient.
He who hesitates is lost.
He who laughs last laughs best.
He who marries for money earns it many times over.
He who will dance must pay the fiddler.
He won't fall for that again.
Heads I win, tails you lose.
Heads will roll.
Health is better than wealth.
Heap coals of fire on his head.
Heaven has no rage like love to hatred turned, nor hell a fury like a woman scorned!
Heavens to Betsey.
Heavy, heavy, hangs over the head.
He'd give me the shirt off his back.
Hell hath no fury lie a woman's scorn.
Hell is paved with good intentions.
He'll get paid back alright.
He'll never set the world on fire.
He'll swing for it.
Hello and Goodbye.
Hell's bells.
Helter skelter.
Her name is on the tip of my tongue.
Her tongue is a rattle trap.
Here, there, and everywhere.
Here I am world, deal with me.
Here's your hat, what's your hurry.
He's a bad egg.
He's a big drip.
He's a book worm.
He's a bully.
He's a cheap skate.
He's a dead beat.
He's a fifth wheel.
He's a globe trotter.
He's a good old soul.
He's a henpecked husband.

He's a horses neck.
He's a lame brain.
He's a little pill.
He's a living doll.
He's a nut.
He's a pain in the neck.
He's a panty-waist.
He's a rich old geezer.
He's a road hog.
He's a round peg in a square hole.
He's a sad sack.
He's a sitting duck.
He's a snake in the grass.
He's a sour dough.
He's a southpaw.
He's a stool pigeon.
He's a stuffed shirt.
He's a tight wad.
He's a tough old bird.
He's a wet blanket.
He's a wise old owl.
He's about knee-high to a grasshopper.
He's afraid of his own shadow.
He's after his pound of flesh.
He's all washed up.
He's as drunk as a skunk.
He's been under the weather.
He's blind in one eye and can't see out of the other.
He's carrying a chip on his shoulder.
He's cock of the walk.
He's down in the dumps.
He's feeling down in the mouth.
He's feeling his oats.
He's full of hot air.
He's full of wet wash.
He's generous to a fault.
He's going like a house afire.
He's going to the dogs.
He's got a wheel loose in his head.
He's got all the answers.

He's got his Sunday go-to-meeting clothes on.
He's got more brass than a government mule.
He's got spring fever.
He's head over heels in love.
He's in deep water.
He's in hot water.
He's in the dog house.
He's just a bag of wind.
He's just a big stuffed shirt.
He's just bluffing.
He's just plain cuckoo.
He's like a roaring lion.
He's living in a fool's Paradise.
He's living in the past.
He's living the life of Riley.
He's made a fool of himself.
He's my reason for living.
He's on a spree.
He's on pins and needles.
He's on the grave yard shift.
He's only half baked.
He's out cold.
He's pickled.
He's pulling her chestnuts out of the fire.
He's pulling the cork.
He's riding on the horns of a dilemma.
He's sitting on top of the world.
He's sitting straddle on the fence.
He's sleeping with one eye open.
He's slick as grease.
He's sowing his wild oats.
He's the life of the party.
He's three sheets to the wind.
He's true blue.
He's trying to lead me into a trap.
He's trying to pump me.
He's twisting the truth.
He's under the weather.
He's well heeled.
He's wrapped around her finger.

Hi there!
Hi, toots.
Hi Yo Silver, Away.
Hiding in plain site.
High and mighty, holier than thou.
High as a kite.
High jinks.
Hip, hip, hooray.
His bark is worse than his bite.
His eccentricity, etymologically considered is evident.
His eyes are bigger than his stomach.
His finale could have been our ending.
His head is in the clouds.
His mind can hold only one thought at a time.
Hit the deck.
Hit the road.
Hit the road Jack.
Hit the trail.
Hitting below the belt.
Hitting the jackpot.
Hog wash.
Hogging it down.
Hold the fort.
Hold the phone.
Hold your hat.
Hold your horses.
Hold your tongue.
Hold your water, I'm coming.
Holy mackerel.
Holy smoke.
Homelier than a hedge fence.
Honest Abe.
Honest as the day is long.
Honest Injun.
Honesty is the best policy.
Honor the dead by helping the living.
Hook, line and sinker.
Hop on board.
Hop, skip and a jump.
Hop to it.

Hope deferred maketh the heart sick.
Hope springs eternal in the human breast.
Horsing around.
Hot as a fire.
Hot as a furnace.
Hot as a pepper pod.
Hot diggity.
Hot diggity dog.
Hot dog.
Hot under the collar.
Hotter than a firecracker.
Hotter than a pepper pod.
Hotter than hell.
Hotter than Tophet.
How are you?
How do I rate?
How do you do it?
How do you feel today?
How do you get that way?
How do you know he's lying? His lips are moving.
How do you like that?
How many times do I have to tell you?
How much is too much?
How would you like to earn a fast buck?
How you gonna mail it, carrier pigeon?
How'd ya like that?
How's chances?
How's tricks?
Hunky-dory.
Hurrah for the red, white, and blue.
Hurry back.

I

I almost had heart failure.
I am a victim of my circumstances!
I am over the moon.
I am true blue!
I am who I am and that's all that I am.
I before E except after C.
I cannot tell a lie, I cut the tree. George Washington
*I can't find my cell phone.
I can't read your mind.
I can't stomach that.
I could care less.
I could cut out my tongue.
I could do it with a drink.
I could kick myself.
I could lick you with one hand tied behind me.
I could skin him alive.
I could snatch him bald-headed.
I couldn't care less.
I cut my own throat.
I didn't think anything would surprise me.
I don't buy it.
I don't care a jot.
I don't get it.
I don't give a darn.
I don't see the point.
I don't want any trouble.
I fa' down and go boom.
I feel full as a tick.
I feel like a stuffed toad.
I feel rotten.
I felt like falling through the floor.
I gave 'em the raspberry.
I gave him a piece of my mind.
I gave him all I had.
I gave him the slip.
I give up.
I goofed.

I got my nickel's worth.
I gotta grab a little zheezh ish.
I guess there's a first time for everything.
I had him over a barrel.
I had the whole nine yards.
I had to pinch myself to see if I was awake.
I hate the ground he walks on.
I hate the ground she walks on.
I hate you.
I have a bone to pick with you.
I have a crush on him.
I have a hunch.
I have a lunch.
I have a thing or two to say about that.
I have an axe to grind.
I haven't seen you in a coon's age.
I haven't seen you in a dog's age.
I haven't seen you in a month of Sundays.
I haven't the faintest idea.
I haven't the slightest idea.
I haven't the slightest notion.
I hit my funny bone.
I invoke the rule shield of the 5th amendment.
I know what you mean.
I know which side my bread is buttered on.
I know you've been hurt but when are you going to come out of your shell?
I love my wife but oh, you kid.
I love you!
I love you more than anything.
I made a boo boo.
I mean business.
I needed it like I needed a hole in my head.
I never had the slightest intention.
I only work here.
I refuse to answer on the grounds that it may incriminate me.
I respectfully disagree with you.
I see what you mean.
I shook like a leaf.
I should hope to kiss a pig.

I should say not.
I thank you from the bottom of my heart.
I think it's going to rain.
I thought I'd die a laughing.
I thought I'd pass out.
I told you so.
I use to could.
I wanna run something by you first.
I want to call collect.
I want to see him pin her ears back.
I was fit to be tied.
I was just floored.
I was just kidding around.
I was just pulling your leg.
I was right.
I was scared stiff.
I was scared to death.
I was tickled almost to death.
I wasn't her type.
I wish you all the luck.
I wonder if she's got all her buttons.
I went straight to the horse's mouth.
I won't knuckle.
I won't play second fiddle to anyone.
I would if I could.
I wouldn't do it for love or money.
I wouldn't give a nickel for it.
I wouldn't give him nickel if he was starving.
I wouldn't trust him behind my back.
I wouldn't trust him out of my sight.
I wouldn't trust you any farther than I could throw a bull by the tail.
I wouldn't wear that to a dog fight.
I'd be wise as an owl.
I'd burn in Hell first.
I'd have him boiled in oil.
I'd knock him flatter than a pancake.
I'd like to punch him in the nose.
Idle hands are the devil's playthings.
Idle hands are the devil's tools.
Idle hands are the devil's workshop.

If a man goes around with a chip on his shoulder, the chances are that it came off his head.
If at first you don't succeed, try, try again.
If I can't be a good example, I'll be a terrific warning.
If I were rich do you know what I'd do?
If I'm not telling the truth, may lighting strike me.
If it is to be, it is up to me. (ten two letter words)
If it isn't one thing, it's another.
If it was a bee it would have stung you.
If 1 + 1 doesn't equal 2 than it isn't correct.
If that don't take the cake.
If that wouldn't jar you.
If the mountain will not come to Mahomet then Mahomet must go to the mountain.
If the shoe fits, put it on.
If the sun sets red it will be a fair day tomorrow.
If you can't do it right, don't do it.
If you can't lose as graceful as you win, you simply shouldn't gamble.
If you care to drive, drive with care.
If you don't like it, lump it.
If you haven't got it, get it!
If you kill the golden goose, you won't get any more golden eggs.
If you think you can trick me into that, you have another think coming.
If you wait too long you'll miss the boat.
If you wanna keep a man honest, never call him liar.
If you want a thing done, do it yourself.
If you want it done right, do it yourself.
If you'd steal a pen you'd steal a bigger thing.
If you'll lie about one thing, you'll lie about everything.
I'll be a dirty bird.
I'll be a gone goose.
I'll be a monkey's uncle.
I'll be there with bells on.
I'll beat the tar out of you.
I'll bet dollars to doughnuts.
I'll bet my bottom dollar.
I'll bet you a nickel.
I'll bet you ten to one.
I'll bet you 25 to one.
I'll do anything you want me to do.

I'll do it if it kills me.
I'll drink to that!
I'll get even if it takes the rest of my life.
I'll give it a lick and a promise.
I'll go along with that.
I'll have to hand it to you.
I'll leave you to stew in your own juice.
I'll make him eat dirt.
I'll make mince meat of him.
I'll needle him.
I'll never get over it.
I'll play the hand I drew.
I'll pray for you.
I'll say so.
I'll take a chance.
I'll take my hat off to 'em.
I'll take you at your word.
I'll talk your arms off.
I'll tan your hide.
I'll tell the world.
I'll throw you out on your ear.
I'm a regular night hawk.
I'm all ears.
I'm all petered out.
I'm all pooped out.
I'm all shook up.
I'm as stubborn as a mule.
I'm at the end of my rope.
I'm beginning to see the light.
I'm burned up.
I'm coming into some money.
I'm dead on my feet.
I'm feeling in the pink.
I'm flabbergasted.
I'm from Missouri, you'll have to Show Me.
I'm glad to make your acquaintance.
I'm going around in circles.
I'm going to hit the hay.
I'm in a pickle.
I'm in the pink of condition.

I'm in too deep to get out.
I'm just dying to do it.
I'm just keeping my fingers crossed.
I'm just on needles and pins.
I'm knocking on wood.
I'm not going on any wild goose chases.
I'm not just whistling Dixie.
I'm off and running.
I'm on a diet.
I'm on the water wagon.
I'm on the water wagon now.
I'm playing my hunch.
I'm ready brother.
I'm real proud of you.
I'm right on top of it.
I'm sick of waiting for her/him to call me.
I'm so proud of you.
I'm so tired I can hardly think straight.
I'm sticking my neck out.
I'm stuck with it.
I'm taking a chance.
I'm the son of a sea cow.
I'm tickled pink.
I'm tired of waiting for you.
I'm waiting with bated breath and itchy feet.
I'm working in the dark.
In a devil-may-care way.
In a queer sort of way.
In God we trust.
In hot water.
In peace sons bury their fathers. In war, fathers bury their sons.
In spite of all your pains.
In spite of hell and high water.
In the middle of nowhere.
In the spring a young man's fancy lightly turns to thoughts of love.
In the twinkle of an eye.
In the very best of men there is a little bad and in the very worst of
men there is a little good.
Is it worth one's salt?
Is that so?

Is there anything you want to get off your chest?
Is this an episode or a condition?
It almost make me jump out of my skin.
It beats all get out.
It beats the band.
It beats the Devil.
It beats the Dutch.
It boggled my mind.
It bowls me over.
It burns me up.
It came like a shot out of a gun.
It came straight from the horse's mouth.
It can't be beat.
It couldn't be done but the darn fool didn't know it and went ahead and did it anyway.
It fits like an old shoe.
It gets my goat.
It gives me the horrors.
It goes in one ear and out the other.
It has all gone down the drain.
It hit the bottom level.
It is more blessed to give than to receive.
It isn't what you mean to do, it's what you do.
It just doesn't seem to sink in.
It keeps 'em in stitches.
It keeps his nose on the grindstone.
It keeps you on your toes.
It makes a whale of a difference.
It might have been.
It never rains but it pours.
It sent a trill up his leg.
It shines like a diamond in a coal bin.
It smells.
It smells like a high-holder's nest.
It smells to high heaven.
It sounds like music to my ears.
It suits my taste.
It takes a lot of grit.
It takes a steady hand to carry a full cup.
It takes all kinds of people to make a world.

It takes the smart one to play the fool.
It takes two to make a bargain.
It was a shindig.
It was a shoddy trick.
It was a whopper.
It was all a lie.
It was all cut and dried beforehand.
It was just a bad dream.
It was just a slip of the tongue.
It was so close it could have bit you.
It went like greased lightning.
It'll be done before you can skin a rabbit.
It'll put you to sleep like rain on a tin roof.
It's a beautiful day.
It's a breeze.
It's a bug-a-boo.
It's a bum steer.
It's a Chinaman's chance.
It's a cinch.
It's a cooking, Joseph.
It's a delusion and a snare.
It's a dog gone shame.
It's a dog in the manger.
It's a dog's life.
It's a free country.
It's a free-for-all.
It's a hard nut to crack
It's a hop, skip, and a jump.
It's a humdinger.
It's a measly shame.
It's a nice day for the race, ain't it? What race? The human race.
It's a no good hen that cackles in you house and lays in another.
It's a red letter day.
It's a rip snorter.
It's a slap in the face of ______?
It's a squeaky wheel that get the grease.
It's a squeaky wheel that get the oil.
It's a surprise.
It's a tee-hee's nest with a ta-ha's egg in it.
It's a tight squeeze.

It's adding fuel to the fire.
It's all above board.
It's all cut and dried.
It's all in your head or mind.
It's all in your imagination.
It's all over my head.
It's all poppycock.
It's all water over the dam.
It's all wool and a yard wide.
It's an ill wind that blows no good.
It's an old wives tale.
It's as clear as a bell.
It's been ages since I've seen you.
It's better to be a live dog than a dead lion.
It's better to be in a hole than in a rut.
It's better to be late than never.
It's better to be safe than sorry.
It's better to have loved and lost than never to have loved at all.
It's blue Monday.
It's brand new.
It's crystal clear!
It's customary to throw rice.
It's darkest just before the dawn.
It's do or die for me.
It's enough to drive a person to drink.
It's for free.
It's for the birds.
It's free as water.
It's getting late.
It's good enough for government work.
It's greener than grass.
It's hotter than blazes.
It's in the cards.
It's in the offing.
It's just a figment of the imagination.
It's just duck soup to me.
It's just one thing and another.
It's like a bolt of lightning.
It's like finding a rattle snake in you bureau drawer.
It's like pouring sand down a rat hole.

It's like stealing pennies from a dead man's eyes.
It's like taking candy from a baby.
It's like throwing a wet blanket over you.
It's little potatoes.
It's love, it's love, and you can't stop it, the bug has bit you and you've got it.
It's love that makes the world go 'round.
It's money that makes the world go around.
It's moving at a glacial pace.
It's my prediction.
It's never too late to learn.
It's never too late to mend.
It's nice to know what's cooking in the other fellow's kettle.
It's nice weather for ducks.
It's no dice.
It's no joke.
It's no skin off my nose.
It's not over til it's over.
It's not over til you snuff my torch.
It's not worth the paper it's written on.
It's nothing to be sneezed at.
It's on the house.
It's on the level.
It's only gossip.
It's only puppy love.
It's play or pay.
It's possible but not probable.
It's raining cats and dogs.
It's right under your nose.
It's simply out of this world.
It's strictly for the birds.
It's the bees knees.
It's the calm before the storm.
It's the cat's me'ow.
It's the cat's pajamas.
It's the cat's whiskers.
It's the fortunes of war.
It's the funniest thing.
It's the hand writing on the wall.
It's the limit.

It's the little things that count.
It's the living end.
It's the real McCoy.
It's the same old grind.
It's time to draw a line in the sand.
It's too late.
It's top secret.
It's up to you.
It's very plush.
It's what you can learn after you know it's all that counts.
It's worth a gamble.
I've a bone to pick with you.
I've got a frog in my throat.
I've got my work cut out for me.
I've got the blues.
I've got to hand it to you.
I've other fish to fry.
I've no time to fool.
I've reached the end of my rope.
I've told you a dozen times.

J

J6ers
Jack of all trades and master of none.
Jailbird.
Jazz music.
Jealousy is a green-eyed monster.
Jeepers - Creepers.
Jewhillikers.
Jiminy crickets.
Jitterbug kid, shaking himself to death.
Johnny get your gun and sword and pistol, Johnny get your gun and shoot that crow.
Jump for joy.
Just a big blow hard.
Just a dumb bell.
Just a hair.
Just a lot of rubbish.
Just a minute.
Just a pinch.
Just a simple twist of the wrist.
Just a slip of the lip.
Just a slip of the tongue.
Just as simple as 1, 2, 3.
Just as simple as that.
Just believe in someone.
Just chasing rainbows.
*Just do it.
Just imagine.
Just living on a shoestring.
Just keep your nose out of other people's business.
Just "old home town."
Just once in a blue moon.
Just take a tip from me.
Just telling time.
Just the facts ma'am just the facts.
Just twiddling his thumbs.
Just wait a minute.
Just a minute.
Justice for the J6ers.

K

Keep a stiff upper lip.
Keep a thing 7 years and you'll find a use for it.
Keep cool, calm and collected.
Keep going.
Keep it under your hat.
Keep on your pins.
Keep the ball rolling.
Keep to the right.
Keep your eyes and ears open.
Keep your fingers crossed.
Keep your head on a swivel.
Keep your mouth shut.
Keep your nose clean.
Keep your nose on the grindstone.
Keep your nose out of it.
Keep your shirt on.
Keep your thumb out of your mouth.
Keep your wits about you.
Keeping our heads above water.
Keeping the wolf from the door.
Kick him in the shins.
Kids is kids.
Kilroy was here.
Kind words can never die.
Kings X.
Kiss my ass.
Kiss my foot.
Kit and caboodle.
Knock on wood.
Knock his block off.
Knock, knock, Who's there? Kilroy was there.
Knocked up!
Knowing something like the back of your hand.
Knucklehead

L

Lackadaisical.
Lamps do not talk but they do shine.
Land o' Goshen.
Last but not least.
Lawfare
Lay down your arms, surrender now at once.
Lazy as a pet coon.
Lazy bones, lazy bones sitting in the sun. How you going to get your day's work done?
Leave me alone.
Leave no stone unturned.
Lend an ear.
Let a sleeping dog lie.
Let bygones be bygones.
Let it go in one ear and out the other.
Let me get a word in edgewise.
Let me run something by you first.
Let me warn you my fine feathered friend.
Let that be a lesson to you.
Let the chips fall where they may.
Let well enough alone.
Let your conscience be your guide.
Let's bury the hatchet.
Let's eat!
Let's face it.
Let's get the show on the road.
Let's go Brandon.
Let's have it.
Let's have one for the road.
Let's live it up.
Liar, liar, pants on fire.
Light as a feather.
Light as day. Dark as night.
Like a blushing bride.
Like a bull in a china shop!
Like a bump on a log.
Like a cat in a strange garret.
Like a fish out of water.
Like a pig in a poke.

Like a plugged nickel.
Like a snake in the grass.
Like Achilles heel.
Like begets like.
Like climbing a greased pole.
Like cutting a rotten spot out of an apple.
Like father like son.
Like fighting the Devil with fire.
Like finding a needle in a haystack.
Like sitting on a bed of loose feathers.
Like water running off a ducks back.
Limp as a rag.
Little as a minute.
Little birds in their nest agree.
Little, but Oh, my!
Little fishes in the brook.
Live and let live.
Live each day as if it is your last.
Living from hand to mouth.
Living on the fat of the land.
Lo and behold.
Location, location, location.
Lock, stock, and barrel.
Long may you live, happy may you be, Blessed with children, one-hundred and three.
Long on looks and short on brains.
Long time no see.
Look before you leap.
Look into someone's eyes to see their soul.
Look who the cat drug in.
Looking a gift horse in the mouth.
Looking for trouble?
Lord willing and the creek don't rise.
Love is what makes the world go 'round.
Love knows no fear.
Love laughs at locksmiths.
Love of money is the root of all evil.
Love will go where it is sent.
Love your neighbor as yourself.
Lower than a snake.

M

Mad as a hatter or (hare).
Mad as a hornet.
Madder than a hatter.
Make a wish.
Make America Great Again (MAGA)
Make each moment count.
Make hay while the sunshines.
Make the best of a bad bargain.
Making a mountain out of a mole hill.
Man proposes; God disposes.
Man who has head in clouds cannot keep feet on ground unless he very big man.
Man's work is from sun to sun, But woman's work in never done.
Many a word in kindness spoken, has helped to heal a heart that's broken.
Many are called but few are chosen.
Many hands make light the work.
Marines are the soldiers of the Sea.
Marry in haste and repent at leisure.
May Day (May 1st)
May Day (used as an appeal for urgent assistance)
May I have your ear please?
May the best man win.
*May the force be with you.
Mealy mouthed.
Meaner than the Devil.
Meek as a lamb.
Merry Christmas.
Mind is master over matter.
Mind your manners.
Mind your own business.
Mind your P's and Q's.
Mind your P's and Q's and don't wear out your shoes.
Misery loves company.
Money doesn't grow on trees.
Money is the root of all evil.
Money makes the pockets jingle.

Money makes the world go 'round.
Money talks.
More fun than a barrel of monkeys.
More muscle and less brains.
More or less.
Mumbo Jumbo.
Mum's the word.
Murder will out.
Music hath charms to soothe the savage breast.
My back is killing me.
My dogs are tired.
My feet are killing me.
My kingdom for a horse.
My sakes alive.
My stars and garters.

N

National Anthem (The Star-Spangled Banner) *Performed by the J6ers in the DC Gulag.
Nature must take her course.
Neat as a pin.
Necessity is the mother of inventions.
Needles and pins, needles and pins, When a man marries his troubles begin.
Never bite off more than you can chew.
Never draw to an inside straight.
Never fire your musket until you're sure it's well loaded.
Never give up a sure thing for a possibility.
Never is a long, long time.
Never make a mountain out of a mole hill.
Never say can't.
Never say die.
Never start something you can't finish.
Never take more than you can swallow.
Never was and never will be.
Nincompoop.
Nipped in the bud.
Nit picking.
No bigger than your little finger.
No bigger than your thumb.
No buts about it!
No can do.
No holds barred.
No kidding.
No man can serve two masters.
No matter what happens, the show must go on.
No news is good news.
No one needs a smile so much as the one who has none left to give.
No sense hanging around here.
No siree.
No stone left unturned.
No use crying over spilt milk.
No way Jose.
No way! Way!

No where to go and plenty of time to get there.
Nobody does so much mischief in the world as the fool who means
well.
North end of a south bound mule.
Not by a jugful.
Not if I can help it.
Not on your tin-type.
Nothing ventured, nothing gained.
Nothing ventured nothing worn.
Now don't get excited.
Now don't get me wrong.
Now hear this.
Now I've put my foot in it.
Now I've spoken my piece.
Now just keep your shirt on.
Now just wait a minute.
Now or never.
Now the shoe is on the other foot.
Now what have you got up your sleeve.
No what kind of a crack was that?
Now what in tarnation is that?
Now what's in you pate?
Now, you're cooking with gas.
Now you've struck the right note.
Nuts to you.

O

O, my eye.
O, my heavens.
O, piffle.
O, shucks.
Of all sad words of tongue or pen, The saddest are these, it might have been.
Of all the nerve.
Of all things!
Off/On the clock.
Off the cuff.
Often good things come in small packages.
Oh, baloney.
Oh, brother.
Oh, by gee.
Oh, by gosh.
Oh, darn it.
Oh, fiddle.
Oh, fiddle faddle.
Oh, fiddlesticks!
Oh, for Pete's sake.
Oh, forget it.
Oh, gee.
Oh, gee Whiz.
Oh, gosh.
Oh hand it.
Oh, hum.
Oh, hum, Harry, don't ask me to marry.
Oh, is that so?
Oh, just so-so.
Oh, mother pin a rose on me.
Oh, my aching back.
Oh, my soul.
Oh, rats.
Oh, shoot.
Oh, shucks.
Oh, snap out of it.
Oh, that little black mustache.

Oh, thunderation.
Oh, what a tangled web we weave, when first we practice to deceive.
Oh, what's the use, to chew tobacco when you spit away the juice.
Oh, yeah?
Oh, you think you're funny, don't you?
Oh, you're full of prunes.
Old as the hills.
Old soldiers never die.
On Sophie's soft sofa Sophie's sewing short sleeved shirts.
On the count, 1, 2, 3
On the double.
On the level.
On your head or on the ground.
On your honor.
Once and for all.
Once in a blue moon.
Once upon a time.
1, 2, 3, and away they go.
One fellow's guess is as good as another's.
One for the money, Two for the show, Three to get ready, and Four to go.
One good deed leads to another.
One good turn deserves another.
One grain of luck is sometimes worth a whole field of rice.
One hand washes the other.
One lie calls for another.
One man's food is another man's poison.
One of the stiff-necked generation.
One thing at a time.
One thing led to another.
Only a block head.
Only God knows.
Only the brave deserve the fair.
Open your mouth and shut your eyes, And I'll give you something to make you wise.
Opportunity never kicks in the door like temptation does.
Opportunity strikes but once.
Oshkosh, b'gosh.
Our accounts are in the red.
Out like a light.

Out of sight, out of mind.
Out of this world.
Out of the frying pan and into the fire.

P

Paddle your own canoe.
Painting the town red.
Pale as a ghost.
Papa caught them with a hook, Mamma fried them in a pan, Baby ate them like a man.
Pardon me.
Pass out the crying towels.
Passing the buck.
Pay as you go, or enter.
Paying them in their own coin.
Pearls of Wisdom.
Peek-a-boo, I see you.
Penny found heads up is good luck.
Penny wise and pound foolish.
People living in glass houses should never throw stones.
Pep it up a little.
Perk up.
Perk yourself up.
Picking a hickory gad.
Picking up the pieces.
Pie face.
Pieces of eight.
Pig Latin - example - **Jackie** is **Ackiejay** and **m**oney is **oneym**ay
Pinch a penny and hear the Indian yell.
Pinocchio (his nose grew with each lie he told)
Pipe down.
Play it cool.
Playing both ends toward the middle.
Pleased as punch.
Politics is downstream of culture.
Pom pom pull-away, come away or I'll fetch you away.
Pony up.
Poor as a church mouse.
Poor as Job's turkey.
Poppycock!
Possession is nine points of the law.
Possession is nine-tenths of the law.

Power tends to corrupt, and absolute power corrupts absolutely.
Power to him who power exerts.
Practice makes perfect.
Practice what you preach.
Prayer and meditation.
Presto change.
Pretty as a picture.
Pretty is that pretty does.
Pretty please.
Pride goeth before destruction and a haughty spirit before a fall.
Principle before power.
Procrastination is the thief of time.
Proud as a peacock.
Pucker up.
Pull down your dress. You're a big girl now.
Pull yourself up by your boot straps.
Pulling the carpet right out from under his feet.
Pure as a lily.
Put a bow on it.
Put down your John Henry.
Put 'em both in a bag and shake and see who comes out on top.
Put it down in black and white.
Put on the old feed bag.
Put that in your pipe and smoke it.
Put this on your noggin.
Put up your dukes.
Put your bib and tucker on.
*Put your mask on.
Put'er there.
Putting all of your eggs in one basket.
Putting it across.
Putting on an act.
Putting on the dog.
Putting the best foot forward.
Putting the cart before the horse.
Putting two and two together.

Q

Q and A.
Que Sera Sera - whatever will be, will be.
Quick as a wink or flash.
Quicker than a cat can wink his eye.
Quicker than lightning.
Quicker than scat.
Quit rocking the boat.
Quit your kidding.

R

Rainbow at morn, sign of a storm, rainbow at night, sailor's delight.
Raise a ruckus tonight.
Raising the Devil.
Raking him over the coals.
Reading the riot act.
Reading the writing on the wall.
Ready for chow.
Ready to go off the deep end.
Red and yellow, kiss a fellow.
Red as a beet.
Red as a cherry.
Reduced to the point of absurdity.
Relax!
Remember, anything you say may be held against you.
Remember - As you slide down the bannister of life, don't get a splinter in your career.
Republican's hold office, Democrat's hold power.
Reputation is something that is easier to live up to than it is to live down.
Rest and digest.
Resting on his laurels.
Riches often take wings.
Ride him out on a rail.
Riding piggy-back.
Right off the bat.
Ring off.
Robbing Peter to pay Paul.
Rock 'n roll.
Rolling in clover.
Rome wasn't built in a day.
Roses are red, Violets are blue, Sugar is sweet and so are you.
Rough and ready.

S

Sacred cow.
Saint Patrick's Day in the marnin'.
Sakes alive.
Salute the flag!
Save the pennies, they make the dollars.
Save your breath.
Saving for a rainy day.
Say cheese.
Say exactly what you mean!
Say what you mean and mean what you say.
Says you.
Scarce as hens teeth.
Scarer than hen's teeth.
Search me.
Search your brains.
See through the noise.
See what I mean?
See ya, don't want to be ya.
See you in a second.
See you later alligator, after while crocodile.
Seeing eye to eye.
Seeing is believing.
Semper Fi, Semper Fidelis, Always Faithful.
September morn.
Seven come eleven.
Shake a leg.
Shake it up baby.
Shake, rattle and roll.
Shame on you.
Shape up or ship out.
Share the wealth.
Sharp as a razor.
She can't boil water without burning it.
She can't sing for sour grapes.
She doesn't know if she's coming or going.
She double-crossed you.
She drinks like a fish.

She eats like a bird.
She fell like a ton of bricks.
She flew off the handle.
She has a bee in her bonnet.
She has bees in her bonnet.
She has her cap set for him.
She screams bloody murder.
She should have her head examined.
She sings like a bird.
She smokes like a chimney.
She sure knows her onions.
She tells little white lies.
She went off the deep end.
She wore the pants in the family.
She works like a horse.
She's a big chump.
She's a cute little dish.
She's a dizzy dame.
She's a giggler.
She's a high stepper.
She's a little devil.
She's a living doll.
She's a peach.
She's a rip snorter.
She's as happy as a clam.
She's 40 if she's a day.
She's got a face that would stop an eight day clock.
She's homely as a hedge fence.
She's like a china doll.
She's my pin up girl.
She's pulling the wool over his eyes.
She's so stuck up.
She's some tomato.
She's such a clinging vine.
Shiny as a new penny.
Ship ahoy.
Shiver my timbers.
Shoot to kill.
Shooting from the hip.
Shooting off your mouth.

Shooting the bull.
Show and tell.
Shut your mouth.
Shut your trap.
Sick as a horse.
Sicker than a dog.
Sign in, please.
Sign up.
Silence is golden.
Simmer down.
Sin is the transgression of the law.
Since you've gone away.
Sit still, you're rocking the boat.
Size doesn't matter.
Skedaddle!
Skinny as a bean pole.
Skip it.
Sleeping with his boots on.
Slick as a mitten.
Slippery as an eel.
Slow as a snail.
Slow down and breathe.
Slower than molasses in January.
Slower traffic keep right.
Sly as a fox.
Smart Alec!
Smart as a whip.
Smashed to smithereens.
Smile and the world smiles with you, weep and you weep alone.
Smooth as glass.
Smooth as silk.
Snap out of it.
Snug as a bug in a rug.
So, do you want to make something of it?
So help me God.
So what?
So you had to pop off.
So you say.
Sober as a judge.
Sodom and Gomorrah.

Soft as a kitten.
Soft as down.
Some laugh to forget, others forget to laugh.
Some like it hot.
Some things weren't meant to be.
Sooner said than done.
Sounding off.
Sour as a pickle or lemon.
Spare the rod and spoil the child.
Speak softly and carry a big stick.
Speak the truth and shame the devil.
Speak when you're spoken to.
Spick and span.
Stand up for your own rights.
Start off on the right foot.
Starting from scratch.
Starting with a shoe string.
Starve a fever and feed a cold.
Step on it.
Stick 'em up.
Stick to your knitting.
Stick to your own belief.
Stick to your own guns.
Sticks and stones may break my bones but words will never hurt me.
Sticking your neck out.
Stiff as a poker.
Still as a mouse.
Still putting in on, eh?
Still water runs deep.
Stop and go.
Straight as a string.
Straight from the horse's mouth.
Strain at a gnat and swallow a camel.
Strike while the iron is hot.
Strong as an ox.
Stubborn as a mule.
*Success will bring us together. Donald J. Trump
Such a highty tighty.
Sugar coated.
Sugar is sweet and so are you.

Sunny side of the street.
Sure as you're born.
Sure thing.
Swallow your pride.
*Swamp the vote.
Sweep your own doorstep first before trying to sweep another's.
Sweet patootie.
Sweet sixteen and never been kissed.
Sweeter than honey.
Sweeter than the day before.
Swift as the wind.

T

Take a deep breath!
Take a load off your feet.
Take a run for yourself.
Take a spoon and you'll get more.
Take care of the little things and the big things will take care of
themselves.
Take it easy now.
Take it with a grain of salt.
Take time by the forelock.
Take you choice.
Take your pick.
Taking a coffee break.
Taking the bull by the horns.
Talk about the angels and you'll hear their wings flutter.
Talk is cheap but it takes money to buy whiskey.
Talk of the devil and he's sure to appear.
Talk to the hand.
Talking your arm off.
Tally ho!
Tattle tale, tattle tale.
Tee for two.
Teeter totter, bread and water.
Tell a secret to one and the world will soon know it.
Tell it to the Marines.
Tell me the truth.
Tell the truth and shame the Devil.
Thank goodness.
Thank your lucky stars.
Thanks for the buggy ride.
That can change in a heart beat.
That cuts no ice.
That cuts no ice with me.
That doesn't make horse sense.
That gets under my skin.
That hand that rocks the cradle rules the world.
That hit my funny bone.
That hit you right between the eyes.

That hits the right spot.
That sounds corny.
That sure cuts across the grain.
That takes the cake.
That was a close shave.
That was a lucky break.
That was sporting of you.
That went over like a lead balloon.
That wets my appetite.
That wraps it up.
That'll make hair grow on your chest.
That'll take her down a peg or two.
That's a big yarn.
That's a cat of a different color.
That's a cottonpicken' lie!
That's a hard nut to crack.
That's a horse of a different color.
That's a hot potato.
That's a lot of baloney.
That's a lot of hog wash.
That's a lot of water under the bridge.
That's a phase he's going through.
That's about the size of it.
That's all out of date.
That's an order!
That's another breed of cats.
That's corny.
That's enough to scare the pants off from anyone.
That's how the banana splits.
That's how the hair splits.
That's how the shoe pinches.
That's how the world goes.
That's just a lot of hot air.
That's just a new fangled notion.
That's just an old wives tale.
That's just an old woman's whim.
That's just chicken feed.
That's just like a man.
That's just what's going to happen.
That's more than I can swallow.

That's my line.
That's my middle name.
That's no skin off my teeth.
That's O.K.
That's on the level.
That's one for the books.
That's one thing for sure.
That's only a drop in the bucket.
That's pretty far-fetched.
That's rich.
That's right down my alley.
That's some fish story.
That's something they cooked up.
That's straight from the heart.
That's terrific.
That's the best I've heard yet.
That's the deadline.
That's the idea.
That's the last straw.
That's the long and the short of it.
That's the one that got away.
That's the score.
That's the stuff.
That's the straw that broke the camel's back.
That's the way Niagara Falls.
That's the way the butter flies.
That's the way the clock runs.
That's the way the cookie crumbles.
That's the way the corn pops.
That's the way the nut cracks.
That's water under the bridge.
That's what I told you.
That's where reason went out the window.
The Age of Deception.
The apple of his eye.
The best laid plans of mice and men oft go astray.
The best things in life are free.
The better the day the better the deed.
The big apple.
The big bad wolf.

The big bully.
The bloody English.
The brazen hussy.
The cat's pajamas.
The cat's whiskers.
The Charleston.
The cheap skate.
The clock is ticking.
The court of last resort.
The Cubanola glide.
The devil finds work for idle hands to do.
The devil's to pay.
The die is cast.
The difficult is easy but the impossible is a little harder.
The dirty Dutch.
The early bird catches the worm.
The early bird gets the worm.
The End.
The end justifies the means.
The end of time.
The end will suffice the means.
The fat is in the fire.
The few, the proud, the Marines.
The filthy rich.
The first one hundred years is the hardest.
The frenzied Frenchman frequently fretted over fickle freckled faced
Freddy.
The fruit doesn't fall far from the tree that bears it.
The ghost walks.
The grass is always greener on the other side of the fence.
The hand is quicker than the eye.
The hand that rocks the cradle rules the world.
The heat is on.
*The Indianapolis pace car.
The jerk.
The least said the soonest mended.
The letter S turns miles into smiles.
The light begins to dawn.
The little black book.
The little foxes spoil the vines.

The longest way 'round is the sweetest way home.
The luck of the draw.
The moon is made of green cheese.
The more haste the less speed.
The more the merrier.
The more you eat the more you want.
The odds are against us.
The pen is mightier than the sword.
The Power of Positivity.
The proof's in the pudding.
The proof of the pudding is in the eating.
The race is not only to the swift nor the battle to the strong.
The Rasz-ma-tazz.
The red, white, and blue.
The Rest of the Story. (Paul Harvey)
The road to hell is paved with good intentions.
The saddest are these - it might have been.
The shortest distance between two points is a straight line.
The sky's the limit.
The straw that broke the camel's back.
The tongue is mightier than the sword.
The ugly American.
The victim was hogtied.
The way to a man's heart is through his stomach.
The whole kit and kaboodle.
The whole story was made up out of whole cloth.
The worry wart.
The worst case of indigestion is caused by eating your own words.
Their marriage went on the rocks.
Then to top it all off.
There is a method in his madness.
There is a time and a place.
There is even honor among thieves.
There never was and never will be.
There's a first time for everything.
There's a time for all things.
There's a wheel loose in his head.
There's always a thorn between conscience and expediency.
There's always final curtain.
There's bats in your belfry.

There's even honor among thieves.
There's more than one way to skin a cat.
There's no business like your own business.
There's no buts about it.
There's no cause for alarm.
There's no fool like the old fool.
There's no man like my Uncle Sam.
There's no place like home.
There's no rest for the wicked.
There's no time like the present.
There's none so blind as those who will not see.
There's nothing new under the sun.
There's one born every minute and two to take him.
There's something I have to get off my chest.
There's something rotten in Denmark.
They are gaslighting you!
They are lying to you!
They are pulling the wool over your eyes.
They couldn't see the forest for the trees.
They dropped me like a hot potato.
They go stringing along.
They got more than they bargained for.
*They indict, we unite.
They left with their tails between their legs.
They lived happily ever after.
They may get wind of it.
They never did it that way in my time.
They never listen.
They said it couldn't be done but he did it.
They that know no evil will suspect none.
They won't see me for dust.
They're as like as two peas in a pod.
They're running me ragged.
They're sure raising heck.
Thin as a rail.
Thin as a wafer.
Things done by halves are never done right.
Think before you speak.
Think Big.
Think twice before you speak.

Thinking about popping the question?
Thirsty as a sponge.
This is a red-letter day.
This is where we came in.
This steak is tough as the sole of my shoe.
Thou shall not kill.
Three cheers for auld Ireland.
Three coins in a fountain.
Three times and out.
Throw the book at him.
Throw the horse over the fence. There's more hay.
Throwing caution to the wind.
Tight as a drum.
Time and tide wait for no man.
Time will tell.
Tired as a dog.
Tit for tat, you kill my dog and I'll kill your cat.
To bear witness to the truth.
To err is human, to forgive is divine.
To heck with it.
To the devil with you.
Toe the line.
Toe the line, or mark.
Toe your mark, get set, go!
Tomorrow is another day.
Tomorrow may be too late.
Tomorrow never comes.
Too beautiful for words.
*Too big to rig.
Too hot for comfort.
Too many cooks spoil the broth.
Too much water has gone over the dam.
Toot your own horn.
Top of the mornin' to ye.
Tossing it around like a hot brick.
Tossing it around like a hot potato.
Tough as a pine knot.
Tougher than leather.
Tougher than tripe.
Trial and error.

Trick or treat.
Trickle down economics.
Tripping the light fantastic.
*True that.
Trump card.
Truth is stranger than fiction.
Trying to keep the wolf away from the door.
Trying to make ends meet.
Turnabout is fair play.
Turn over a new leaf.
Turning the tables on 'em.
23, Skiddoo.
Two can live as cheaply as one.
Two faced.
Two heads are better than one, even through one be a sheephead.
Two minds with but a single thought.
Two State delusion.
Two State solution.
Two wrongs don't make a right.
Two's company, three's a crowd.

U

Ugly as a witch.
Up in the air about it.
Up to his neck in trouble.
Use a little common sense.
Use a little elbow grease.
Use a little horse sense.
Use some sense.
Use your head.
Use your thinker.

V

Vain as a peacock.
Variety is the spice of life.
Venn Diagram.
Vinegar catches flies.

W

Waist deep in the mud and sleeping in a hayloft.
Wake up and pay for your lodging.
Wake up and smell the coffee.
Walk a mile in my shoes.
Walk the plank.
*WANE (We are not enemies!)
War is cruelty and you cannot refine it.
Warm as toast.
Was my face red?
Watch it.
Watch the birdie.
Watch your step.
Water, pure water, it is the drink for me.
Way down yonder in the paw paw patch.
We all make mistakes.
We are living in The Age of Deception.
We go to bed with the chickens.
We have to take the bitter with the sweet.
We own it free and clear.
We The People.
Weak as a kitten.
Weak as water.
Wear your mask.
Wearing your heart on your sleeve.
Weave and worry.
We'll back it to the hilt.
We'll take home the bacon.
Well, bawl my foot off.
Well, bust my britches.
Well, did you ever.
Well, how'd you like that?
Well, hows about it?
Well, I'll be cow-kicked.
Well, I'll be greased.
Well, that makes sense.
Well, what do you know?
Well, what do you think?

Well, what's on your mind?
Well, wrap me up in buffalo hide.
We're having gobs of fun.
We're in no mans land.
We're in the swim.
We're off like a herd of turtles.
We're starting from scratch.
We's all in the same boat.
Wet your whistle.
Whadda ya know!
What a blockhead.
What a difference a day makes.
What a man.
What a man is not up on, he's down on.
What are you fishing for?
What are you so steamed up about?
What can't be cured must be endured.
What do you care?
What goes on behind the iron curtain?
What goes on behind closed doors?
What goes up must come down. On you head or on the ground.
What happens in Vegas stays in Vegas!
What happens today is inevitably controlled by what has happened in the past.
What in Sam Hill are you doing?
What in the Devil are you doing?
What is a home without a mother?
What is sauce for the goose is sauce for the gander.
What is the dope?
What is your name, rank, and serial number?
What under sun and earth are you doing?
What under the sun are you talking about?
What you are will show in what you do.
What you need is a hobby.
Whatever!
Whatever one can do, two can do better than one.
Whatever you do, do with your might.
What's cooking?
What's eating you?
What's good for the goose is good for the gander.

What's in a name?
What's new?
What's that got to do with the price of eggs?
What's the great idea?
What's the news?
What's the racket?
What's the rumble?
What's the time?
What's the verdict?
What's your game?
When angry, count to ten before you speak.
When in Rome, do as the Romans do.
When my ship comes in.
When the cat's away, the mice will play.
When the shoe is on the other foot.
When the soles of your shoes are thin, if you step on a dime you can
tell if its heads or tails.
When the sun is in the west, lazy people work the best.
When you find a friend that is kind and true, Change not the old one
for the new.
When you indict him you unite US. MAGA
When you wink the other eye.
Where angels fear to tread.
Where are the keys?
Where did you get your manners?
Where do you think you're are going?
Where have you been keeping yourself?
Where ignorant is bliss 'tis folly to be wise.
Where there is a will there is a way.
Where there is life there is hope.
Where there is smoke, there must be some fire.
Where there's a will there's a way.
Where there's life there's hope.
Whistling girls and crowing hens, Always come to dreadful ends.
Whistle pass the graveyard.
White as a sheet.
Who do you think you are?
Who dunit?
Who goes there?
Who knows?

Who wears the pants?
Whoa there, not so fast.
Whole nine yards.
Will you accept a collect call?
Will you love me in December as you do in May?
Will you take my hand?
Win by more, lose by less.
Wise as an owl.
Wish me luck.
Wish upon a star.
Wishy washy.
With the greatest of pleasure.
Without further ado.
Words matter!
Work like a dog.
Work like the Dickens.
Working for peanuts.
Worry nut.
Would that mistakes could be sold for as much as they cost.
Would you like to call collect?
Wouldn't that get your nanny?
Wouldn't that kill you?
Wrap it up!
Wrinkled as a prune.
Why not?

Y

Years may wrinkle the skin, but to give up enthusiasm wrinkles the soul.
Yell it from the house tops.
Yellow as saffron.
You are a brick.
You are as honest as the day is long.
You are nuts.
You are responsible for others safety.
You are so beautiful.
You are to blame.
You aren't getting anywhere fast.
You aren't just whistling Dixie.
You aren't my father/mother.
You Auto Buy now.
You bet your life.
You big fool.
You can bet your bottom dollar.
You can fool some of the people some of the time but you can't fool all of them all of the time.
You can get 'em for a dime a dozen.
You can go to grass.
You can have your cake and eat it too.
You can lead a horse to water but you can not make him drink.
You can say that again.
You can take this job and shove it!
You can't catch a bull by his tail.
You can't catch a fish without bait.
You can't compromise with evil or it may come back and roost on your own doorstep.
You can't get blood out of a turnip.
You can't give with one hand and take with the other.
You can't have your cake and eat it too.
You can't make me!
You can't pump water when the well's gone dry.
You can't see any farther than the end of your nose.
You can't take it with you when you die.
You can't teach an old dog new tricks.

You can't tell a book by it's cover.
You can't tell a man by the clothes he wears.
You can't tell by the looks of a toad how far he can jump.
You can't tell me what to do!
You couldn't touch him with a 10-foot pole.
You dirty rat!
You gave me so much hope.
You give me the heeby jeebies.
You got bamboozled!
You got played.
You have another thing coming.
You have no skin in the game!
You have something up your sleeve.
You haven't seen anything yet.
You heard me.
You knock kneed, bow legged, pigeon toed ninny.
You know?
You little imp.
You little monkey.
You little simpleton.
You little stick in the mud.
You look great for an old geezer.
You look like a ghost.
You look like the cat that swallowed the canary.
You missed it by a mile.
You missed it by inches.
You must be blind.
You must have got out on the wrong side of the bed.
You must sow the seed before you can reap the harvest.
You must win as gracefully as you lose.
You never can tell.
You never know how much you can do until you have to.
You Nitwit.
You offended me.
You ought to have your head examined.
You own it all, lock, stock and barrel.
You said it.
You said it, I didn't.
You send me.
You should have seen the one that got away.

You son of a gun.
You took the words right out of my mouth.
You were right.
You'd better high-tail it.
You'd better simmer down.
You'd better take to the tall timber.
You'd never catch me doing such a thing.
You'll be playing a different tune.
You'll do it over my dead body.
You'll get an earful.
You'll have another kind of laugh coming.
You'll need a Philadelphia lawyer to get you out of that.
You're a bad egg.
You're a girl after my own heart.
You're a knuckle head.
You're a liar.
You're a loser.
You're a sap.
You're a sight for sore eyes.
You're a winner.
You're always hearing things.
You're an old fussbudget.
You're barking up the wrong tree.
You're both ends toward the middle.
You're buttering your bread on the wrong side.
You're chicken.
You're crazy.
You're cutting your nose off to spite your face.
You're foolish.
You're full of gravy.
You're getting in my hair.
You're going to learn something you never learned in a book.
You're just adding more fuel to the flame.
You're just as old as you feel.
You're just frittering your time away.
You're just having a pipe dream.
You're just having daydreams.
You're making a mountain out of a mole hill.
You're not half as smart as you think you are!
You're not the only pebble on the beach.

You're not the only toad in the puddle.
You're old enough to know what you are doing.
You're on the wrong track.
You're right as rain.
You're so right.
You're stretching the truth.
You're the cream in my coffee.
You're the one who got away.
You're the talk of the town.
You're too old-fashioned.
You're under the weather.
You're wasting your time.
You've been lucky.
You've got nothing to live for.
You've got the right shoe on the wrong foot.
You've got to show me.
You've had it.
You've made your bed, now lie in it.
You've sure got a nerve.
Your barn door is open.
Your goose is cooked.
Your guess is as good as mine.
Your head is too big for your hat.
Your picture, is something to scare the rats and mice away.
Your wish is my command.
Youth is not a time of life, it is a state of mind.

Books, Movies, Nursery Rhymes, Trial, TV Shows

I haven't seen all that many movies, especially today's movies. Then there are movies that I have seen many times, like *Gone with the Wind*, *Casablanca*, *A Few Good Men and Cool Hand Luke*. One of the funniest things I can ever remember is Paul Newman eating those 50 hard-boiled eggs.

Being a former Marine I have watched *A Few Good Men* the most, probably 10 times. There are more movies that have been important to me but I can't remember the names and haven't seen them in many years, so I can't quote from them. Therefore, there are only a few movies mentioned below.

TV Shows

O. J. Simpson's trial (1994/95) talking about gloves.

Murders Jun 12, 1994. Trial was in 1995.

It doesn't fit. You must acquit.

If it doesn't fit, you must acquit. (Johnnie Cochran)

The Apprentice (Donald Trump's TV Show)

You're fired.

Robin Hood

a person considered to be taking from the wealthy and giving to the poor.

Wagon Train - The John Augustus Story

Ashes, all that I held dear, ashes. All a man owns really is himself... his own life. And I thought mine was in that wagon. But it's not. If it were, I'd crumple now, I'd be ashes. Instead, I feel suddenly free. Freedom like I've never known before. I thought I owned those works of art, but they possessed me. I allowed myself to be enslaved by them as if by a drug.

Subway Commercial

Five dollar foot long.

Camel Cigarette Commercial

I'd walk a mile for a Camel.

Arby's commercial

Where's the beef?

Movies

<u>A Few Good Men</u> (1992)
I want the truth. You can't handle the truth!

<u>A Streetcar Named Desire</u> (1951)
Stella! Hey, Stella!

<u>Alice in Wonderland</u>
Curiouser and curiouser!
I don't think — Then you shouldn't talk.
If I had a world of my own, everything would be nonsense.
It's no use going back to yesterday, because I was a different person then.
Off with their heads!
We're all mad here.
Who in the world am I? Ah, that's the great puzzle!
Why, sometimes I've believed as many as six impossible things before breakfast.

<u>Apolla 13</u> (1995)
Houston, we have a problem.

<u>Bambi</u> (1942)
Faster, faster, Bambi. Don't look back! Keep running, keep running.
If you can't say somethin' nice, don't say nothin' at all.

<u>Bataan</u> (1943)
All right boys, come and get it.
Come on, come on, suckers, come and get it.
Do I have to put it in writing?
Don't fire until you have a target.
How you gonna mail it, carrier pigeon?
Jitterbug kid, shaking himself to death.
Lay down your arms, surrender now at once.
Put this on your noggin.

__Bonnie and Clyde__ (1967)
We rob banks.

__Casablanca - (1942) Humphrey Bogart__
Here's looking at you, kid.
Louis, I think this is the beginning of a beautiful friendship.
Of all the gin joints in all the towns in all the world, she walks into mine.
Play it, Sam. Play "As Time goes By."
Round up the usual suspects.
We'll always have Paris.

__Cat on a Hot Tin Roof__ (1958)
Didn't you notice a powerful and obnoxious odor of mendacity in the room?
I've got the guts to die. What I want to know is, have you got the guts to live?
Time goes by so fast, nothin' can outrun it.
What makes you so restless, have you got ants in your britches.

__Cool Hand Luke (__1967)
A girl is out washing her car— Hey Lord, whatever I don, don't strike me blind for another couple of minutes.
Why you got to go and say fifty eggs? I thought it was a nice round number. I can eat fifty eggs. Nobody can eat fifty eggs. My boy says he can eat fifty eggs, he can eat fifty eggs. Yeah, but in how long? A hour.
What we've got here is failure to communicate.

__Dirty Dancing (__1987)
Nobody puts Baby in a corner.

__Dirty Harry__ (1971)

You've got to ask yourself one question. Do I feel lucky? Well, do ya, punk?

Dr. No (1963)
Bond, James Bond.

E. T. The Extra Terrestrial (1982)
E. T. phone home

Field of Dreams (1989)
If you build it, they will come.

Forrest Gump (1994)
My mama always said life was like a box of chocolates. You never know what you're gonna get.

Gone with the Wind (1939)
After all, tomorrow is another day**!**
As God is my witness, I'll never be hungry again.
Frankly, my dear, I don't give a damn.

Hud (1963) Paul Newman
Don't go shootin' all the dogs cause one of them's got fleas.
It's like a bolt of lightning.

In the Heat of the Night (1967)
They call me Mister Tibbs!

Jerry Maguire (1996)
Show me the money!

Love Story (1970)
Love means never having to say you're sorry.

Midnight Cowboy (1969)
I'm walking here! I'm walking here!

Network (1976)

I'm as mad as hell, and I'm not going to take this anymore.

Saturday Night Fever (1977)
Nice move. Did you make that up? Yeah, well I saw it on TV first,
then I made it up.

Seven Year Itch (1955)
Do you feel the breeze from the subway? Isn't it delicious! It sort
of cools the ankles, doesn't it?
When it gets hot like this, you know what I do? I keep my undies in
the icebox!

Shane (1953)
Shane. Shane. Come back!

She Done Him Wrong (1933) Mae West
Why don't you come up sometime and see me?

Some Like it Hot (1959)
I'm Osgood Fielding the third. I'm Cinderella the second.
Real diamonds, they must be worth their weight in gold.
We won't breathe a word. You won't breathe nothin', no even air.

Star Wars (1972)
May the Force be with you.

Sudden Impact (1983)
Go ahead, make my day.

Taxi Driver (1976)
You talking to me?

Terminator (1984)
I'll be back.

Terminator 2 - Judgment Day (1991)
Hasta la vista, baby.

The Adventures of Sherlock Holmes (1939)
Elementary, my dear Watson.

The Dirty Dozen (1967)
We still have one operation to go. I you guys foul up on this one, none of us will ever play the violin again.
What's your name soldier? Number two, Sir!
You've seen a general inspecting troops before haven't you? Just walk slow, act dumb and look stupid.

The Giant (1956)
Money isn't everything, Jett. Not when you've got it.
You insulted my wife, and you're gonna answer for it.
You're my wife now honey, you're a Benedict.

The Godfather (1972)
I'm gonna make him an offer he can't refuse.

The Godfather Part II (1974)
Keep your friend close, but your enemies closer.

The Graduate (1967)
Mrs. Robinson, you're trying to seduce me. Aren't you?

The Green Mile (1999)
"Catch them young." became my motto.
He killed them with their love.
I'm in heaven!
That's how it is every day all over the world.

The Naughty Nineties (1945)
Who's on first.

The Rack (1956)
I just say, that no matter what a man is supposed to have done, the one that is going to prosecute him has to look into his own soul.

Is there anything I can do for you now?
Maybe there's some special thing you'd like to get off your chest.

The River of No Return (1954)
The Indians call it the River of No Return, from here on, you'll find out why.
Why did you name me Mark? Simple, I'm Matthew. Mark follows Matthew. It's the Bible.

The Sixth Sense (1999)
I see dead people.

The Maltese Falcon (1941)
The stuff that dreams are made of.

The Wizard of Oz (1939)
I'll get you, my pretty, and your little dog, too!
There's no place like home.
Toto, I've a feeling we're not in Kansas anymore.

Titanic (1997)
I'm the king of the world!

Tootsie (1982)
Bulls are bulls and roosters don't try to lay eggs.

Top Gun (1986)
I feel the need, the need for speed!

Wife vs. Secretary (1936)
You should never see the husband.

Other Sayings

sk not what your country can do for you but what can you do for your country. President Kennedy on January 20, 1961, as he became the 35th President of the United States.

Basement dwellers and Basket of deplorables. Hillary Clinton

Do you swear, the evidence you shall give in this case, will be the truth, the whole truth and nothing but the truth, so help you God?

Fee fie fo fum, I smell the blood of an Englishman. Be he alive or be he dead, I'll grind his bones to make my bread.

Friendship is like china, precious, rich and rare, which, once that it is broken, you never can repair.

Fuzzy Wuzzy was a bear. Fuzzy Wuzzy had no hair. Fuzzy Wuzzy wasn't really fuzzy, Fuzzy?

Give me liberty or give me death. Patrick Henry

Give me your tired, your poor, your huddled masses yearning to breathe free!

God has chosen the foolish things of the world to confound the wise, the weak things to confound the strong.

If all the land were pie and cake, and all the sea were ink, and all the trees were bread and cheese, what would the people drink? It's enough to make an old man scratch is head and think.

If you would true wisdom seek, five things observe with care; to whom you speak, of whom you speak, and how and when and where.

John Jacob Jingleheimer Schmidt! His name is my name, too. Whenever we go out, the people always shout! There goes John Jacob Jingleheimer Schmidt.

Neither snow nor rain nor heat or gloom of night stays these couriers from the swift completion of their appointed rounds.

Rich man, poor man, beggar man, thief, doctor, lawyer, Indian chief.

Something Mark Twain said about his father. "When I was 18, I was always embarrassed by what a fool my father was. When I was 21, I was surprised to see how much the old man had learned in three years."

The boy stood on the burning deck, eating peanuts by the peck. His father called but he wouldn't go, because he loved the peanuts so.

The Goose that Laid the Golden Eggs. If you kill the golden goose you don't get any more golden eggs.

The only difference between stumbling blocks and stepping stones is the way you use them.

The presumption of innocence is a legal principle that every person accused of any crime is considered innocent until proven guilty.

The woman who tells her age is either too young to have anything to lose, or too old to have anything to gain.

There's a bedbug on your collar, baby mine. If you pinch him he will holler, baby mine. And then what a smell will holler, baby mine.

When intelligent people hear a wise saying, they applaud it and add to it. When fools hear it, they sneer at it and throw it away.

Nursery Rhymes

A diller a dollar
A diller a dollar, a ten o'clock scholar, what makes you come so soon?
You used to come at ten o'clock, but now you come at noon.

A Tisket, a tasket
A tisket a tasket, A green and yellow basket.
I wrote a letter to my love, and on the way, I dropped it.
I dropped it, I dropped it, and on the way, I dropped it.
A little boy picked it up, and put it in his pocket.

Baa Baa Black Sheep
Baa baa black sheep have you any wool? Yes, sir, Yes, sir, Three bags full.
One for my master, one for my dame, one for the little boy who lives down the land.
Baa baa black sheep have you any wool? Yes, sir, yes, sir, Three bags full.

Bumble Bee, Bumble Bee
Bumble bee, bumble bee, Came from the farm.
and stung little Johnny, right under the arm.

Hey, diddle, diddle
Hey diddle, diddle, the cat in the fiddle.
The cow jumped over the moon,
The little dog laughed to see such a sport,
And the dis ran away with the spoon.

Humpty Dumpty sat on a wall
Humpty Dumpty sat on a wall,
Humpty Dumpty had a great fall;
All the king's horses and all the king's men
Couldn't put Humpty together again.

I wish I was a rock
I wish I was a rock a-sitting on a hill, doing nothing all day, just a sittin' still.
I wouldn't eat, I wouldn't sleep, I wouldn't even wash.
I'd just sit still a thousand years and rest myself, by gosh.

It's Raining, It's Pouring
It's raining, it's pouring, the old man is snoring.
He bumped his head and went to bed, and didn't get up till morning.

Jack and Jill
Jack and Jill went up the hill to fetch a pail of water;
Jack fell down and broke his crown, and Jill came tumbling after.
Up Jack got, and home did trot as fast as he could caper;
He went to bed to mend his head, with vinegar and brown paper.

Jack Be Nimble
Jack be nimble, Jack be quick, Jack jumped over the candlestick.
Jack jumped high, Jack jumped low, Jack jumped over and burned his toe.

Ladybug, Ladybug
Ladybug, ladybug, fly away home, your house is on fire and your children will burn.
The pot is boiling without any meat, and your children are crying for something to eat.

Little Bo-Peep
Little Bo-Peep has lost her sheep and doesn't know where to find them;
Leave them along, and they'll come home, wagging their tails behind them.

Little Boy Blue
Little Boy Blue, come blow your horn. The sheep's in the meadow; the cow's in the corn. Where is the little boy who looks after the sheep? He's under a haystack fast asleep.

Little Jack Horner
Little Jack Horner, sat in the corner, eating a Christmas pie;

He put in his thumb and pulled out a plum, and said, "What a good
boy am I!"

Little Miss Muffet
Little Mis Muffet sat on a tuffet, eating her curds and whey;
There came a big spider who sat down beside her and frightened
Miss Muffet away.

London Bridge Is Falling Down
London Bridge is falling down, falling down, falling down,
London Bridge is falling down, my fair lady.
Take the key and lock her up, lock her up, lock her up
Take the key and lock her up, my fair lady.

Mary, Mary, Quite Contrary
Mary, Mary, quite contrary, how does your garden grow?
With silver bells and cockle-shells and pretty maids all in a row.

Monday's Child is Fair of Face
Monday's child is fair of face,
Tuesday's child is full of grace,
Wednesday's child is full of woe,
Thursday's child has far to go.
Friday's child is loving and giving,
Saturday's child works hard for a living,
And the child that is born on the Sabbath Day,
is bonny and blithe and good and gay.

Old King Cole
Old King Cole was a merry old soul, and a merry old soul was he;
He called for his pipe and he called for his bowl, and he called for
his fiddler three.

One, two, buckle my shoe
One two, buckle my shoe.
Three four, shut the door.
Five six, pick up sticks.
Seven eight, lay them straight.
Nine ten, the big fat hen.

One, two, three, four, five, six, seven
One, two, three, four, five, six, seven, all good children go to heaven.
Eight, nine, ten, eleven, twelve, All bad children to - well?

Pat-A-Cake
Pat-a-cake, pat-a-cake, baker's man, bake me a cake as fast as you can.
Roll it and pat it and mark it with a B, and throw it in the oven for baby and me.

Peter Piper
Peter Piper picked a peck of pickle peppers.
A peck of pickle peppers Peter Piper picked.
Now if Peter Piper picked a peck of pickle peppers
Where is the peck of peppers that Peter Piper picked?

Popcorn
Pip, pop, hip, hop, tip, top popcorn, out of the pan, into the fire,
bursting and bouncing higher and higher, White as new snow,
yellow as gold, you'd better be patient until it is cold.

Rain
Rain, rain go away, Little Sammi want to play.
Rain, rain go away, come again some other day.

Red Rover, Red Rover
Red Rover, Red Rover
Let (person) come over.

Ring Around the Rosy
Ring around the rosy, a pocket full of posies.
Ashes! Ashes! We all fall down.

Rock-A-Bye
Rock-a-bye, Baby, upon the tree top, when the wind blows the cradle will rock.
When the bough breaks the cradle will fall, down crumbles cradle, baby and all.

Row Your Boat
Row, row, row your boat gently down the stream.
Merrily, merrily, merrily merrily life is but a dream.

Rub-a-dub-dub
Rub-a-dub-dub, three men in a tub, and who do they think the be?
The butcher, the baker, the candlestick maker, all of them out to sea.

Star Light Star Bright
Star light, Star bright, first star I see tonight.
I wish I may, I wish I might, have the wish I wish tonight.

The Mouse and the Clock
Hickory, hickory, dock! The mouse ran up the clock.
The clock struck one and down he ran. Hickory dickory dock!

The Spider to the Fly
Won't you come into my parlor, said the spider to the fly.
It's the cutest little parlor that ever you did spy.

There was an Old Woman
There was an old woman who lived in a shoe.
She had so many children she didn't know what to do.
She gave them some broth without any bread,
and whipped them all soundly and put them to bed.

Thirty Days Hath September
Thirty days hath September, April, June, and November, All the rest
have thirty-one, Except February, twenty-eight days clear, And
twenty-nine in each leap year.

Three Blind Mice
Three blind mice, three blind mice, see how they run, see how they run?
They all ran after the farmer's wife, who cut off their tails with a
carving knife,
Did you ever see such a thing in your life, as three blind mice?

Twinkle Twinkle Little Star
Twinkle Twinkle Little Star, how I wonder what you are.
Up above the world so high, like a diamond in the sky.
Twinkle twinkle little star, how I wonder what you are.

Shakespeare

Shakespeare was responsible for many of the things we say today. I would guess that no-one could know all that he was responsible for, but these are a few of them. There are many more plays as well.

<u>A Comedy of Errors</u>
neither rhyme nor reason

<u>Antony and Cleopatra</u>
salad days

<u>As You Like It</u>
forever and a day
too much of a good thing
we have seen better days

<u>Cymbeline</u>
catch a cold
I have not slept one wink

<u>Hamlet</u>
I must be cruel, only to be kind
flesh and blood
in my hearts of hearts
method to his madness
my own flesh and blood
the clothes make the man
though this be madness, yet there is method in it (There's method in my madness)
to thine own self be true (be true to yourself)

Henry IV
give the devil his due
he hath eaten me out of house and home
send him packing
set my teeth on edge

Henry V
a heart of gold
devil incarnate

Henry VI
Dead as a door nail
faint-hearted
mum's the word

Julius Caesar
a dish fit for the Gods
it's all Greek to me
made of sterner stuff

King Henry III
for goodness' sake

King John
fair play
fight fire with fire
play fast and loose

King Lear
full circle

Love's Labour Lost
laugh yourself into stitches
naked truth
zany

Macbeth
come what, come may
knock, knock who's there?
milk of human kindness

one full swoop
something wicked this way comes
the be-all and the end-all
what's done is done

<u>Measure for Measure</u>
refuse to budge an inch

<u>Much Ado About Nothing</u>
lie low

<u>Othello</u>
foregone conclusion
I will wear my heart upon my sleeve
jealousy is the green-eyed monster
neither here nor there
wear my heart upon my sleeve
wear your heart on your sleeve

<u>Richard II</u>
spotless reputation

<u>Richard III</u>
a tower of strength
short shrift

<u>Romeo and Juliet</u>
star-crossed lovers
a wild-goose chase

<u>The Comedy of Errors</u>
neither rhyme nor reason

<u>The Tempest</u>
brave new world
fair play
I have been in such a pickle
melted into thin air
such stuff as dreams are made on

<u>The Merchant of Venice</u>
a blinking idiot
all that glitters isn't gold
love is blind
but in the end truth will out
with bated breath

<u>The Merry Wives of Windsor</u>
as good luck would have it
laughing-stock
the world is mine oyster
the world is your oyster

<u>The Taming of the Shrew</u>
all of a sudden
breaking the ice
kill with kindness
refuse to budge an inch

<u>Titus Andronicus</u>
devil incarnate

<u>Troilus and Cressida</u>
fair play
good riddance

<u>Twelfth Night</u>
laugh one self into stitches

President George Washington

He was our country's first president. I believe he played a great part in the founding of our country. I really admired him. He was very wise and said many wise things. I have picked a couple of the really great ones.

...a good moral character is the first essential in a man...It is therefore highly important that you should endeavor not only to be learned but virtuous.

A sensible woman can never be happy with a fool.

Few men have virtue to withstand the highest bidder.

For although we cannot avoid first impressions we may assuredly place them under guard.

Gentlemen, you will permit me to put on my spectacles, for, I have grown not only gray, but almost blind in the service of my country.

Having now finished the work assigned me, I retire from the great theatre of action.

I hope I shall possess firmness and virtue enough to maintain what I consider the most enviable of all titles, the character of an honest man.

I retain an unalterable affection for you, which neither time or distance can change.

I shall make it the most agreeable part of my duty to study merit, and reward the brave and deserving.

If freedom of speech is taken easy, then dumb and silent we may be led, like sheep to the slaughter.

It is better to offer no excuse than a bad one.

It is infinitely better to have a few good men, than many indifferent ones.

It is our true policy to steer clear of permanent alliance with any portion of the foreign world.

Let your heart feel for the afflictions and distress of everyone, and let your hand give in proportion to your purse.

Liberty, when it begins to take root, is a plant of rapid growth.

Real men despise battle, but will never run from it.

Respect for its authority, compliance with its laws, acquiescence in its measures, are duties enjoined by the fundamental maxims of true liberty.

The Constitution is the guide which I never will abandon.

The foolish and wicked practice of profane cursing and swearing is a vice so mean and low that every person of sense and character detests and despises it.

The harder the conflict, the greater the triumph.

The time is near at hand which must determine whether Americans are to be free men or slaves.

The very idea of the power and the right of the people to establish government presupposes the duty of every individual to obey the established government.

To be prepared for war is one of the most effectual means of preserving peace.

Truth will ultimately prevail where there is pains to bring it to light.

We must consult our means rather than our wishes.

We should not look back unless it is to derive useful lessons from past errors, and for the purpose of profiting by dearly bought experience.

Worry is the interest paid by those who borrow trouble.

Bible

The following are some of my favorite verses in the Bible. I am listing the books of the Bible in order. That's because it's the way I think it should be done but also because those who read the Bible will find a book is easier to find. Another reason is because if you are new to the Bible, you will be learning the order of the books in the Bible.

Also, I am using the Catholic Bible which has seven additional books. Those books are noted by an *. Sometimes you will see a section that only lists one verse. You may have to read several more verses to complete the subject. If you don't already have a Bible, please get one and start your journey to wisdom, world history, God's love for Israel, Israel's boundary and so much more.

Old Testament

Genesis 1: 31 Then God looked over all He had made, and he saw that it was very good.

2:16-17 You may freely eat the fruit of every tree in the garden, except the tree of the knowledge of good and evil.

6:19 Bring a pair of every kind of animal, a male and a female, into the boat with you to keep them alive during the flood.

12:3 I will bless those who bless you, and curse those who treat you with contempt.

22:17 I will multiply your descendants beyond number, like the stars in the sky and the sand on the seashore.

28:15 I will protect you wherever you go.

50:24 He will bring you back to the land he solemnly promised.

Exodus 3:14 I am who I am.

14:14 The Lord himself will fight for you. Just stay calm.

19:5 If you will obey me and keep my covenant, you will be my own special treasure from among all the people on earth.

20:1-17 **The Ten Commandments I** am the Lord your God. You must not have any other god but me. **II** You must not make for yourself an idol of any kind. **III** You must not misuse the name of the Lord your God. **IV** Remember to observe the Sabbath day by keeping it holy. **V** Honor your father and mother. Then you will live a long, full life in the land the Lord your God is giving you. **VI You** must not murder. **VII** You must not commit adultery. **VII** You must not steal. **IX You** must not testify falsely against your neighbor. **X** You must not covet.

34:6 I am slow to anger and filled with unfailing love and faithfulness.

39:43 He blessed them.

Leviticus 19:2 You must be holy because I, the Lord your God, am holy.

22:31 You must faithfully keep all my commands by putting them into practice, for I am the Lord.

Numbers 6:24-25 May the Lord bless you and protect you. May the Lord smile on you and be gracious to you.

14:8 It is a rich land flowing with milk and honey.

34:1-15 The boundaries of the land that God gave to the Israelites.

Deuteronomy 5:6-21 Ten Commandments

6:5 You must love the Lord your God with all your heart, all you soul, and all your strength.

7:9 He is the faithful God who lavishes his unfailing love on those who love him and obey his commands.

31:6 Be strong and courageous! For the Lord your God will personally go ahead of you.

Joshua 10:8 Do not be afraid of them, for I have given you victory over them.

13:8-19:51 All the land given to the twelve sons of Israel.

24:15 **Choose** today whom you will serve. But as for me and my house, we will serve the Lord.

Judges 1:1 Judah and Simeon conquer the land

4:1 Deborah becomes Israel's judge

5:31 May those who love you rise like the Sun in all its power!

6:1 Gideon becomes Israel's judge

13:1 Samson is born

13:5 He will begin to rescue Israel from the Philistines.

14:1 Samson's riddle

16:23 Samson's final victory

Ruth 1:16 Wherever you go, I will go, wherever you live, I will live. Your people will be my people, and your God will be my God.

3:11 Now don't worry about a thing, my daughter.

4:1 Boaz marries Ruth

4:14 Praise the Lord, who has now provided a redeemer for your family!

1 Samuel 2:1 My heart rejoices in the Lord! The Lord has made me strong.

3:10 Speak, your servant is listening.

16:7 The Lord looks at the heart.

17:32-50 David kills Goliath.

30:6 David found strength is the Lord his God.

2 Samuel 7:22 How great you are, O sovereign Lord! There is no one like you.

10:12 May the Lord's will be done.

22:2 The Lord is my rock, my fortress, and my savior.

1 Kings 8:23 God of Israel, there is no God like you in all of Heaven above or on the earth below.

11:38 If you obey my decrees and commands then I will be with you.

2 Kings 2:11 Suddenly a chariot of fire appears, drawn by horses of fire. It drove between the two men separating them, and Elijah was carried by a whirlwind into heaven.

1 Chronicles 4:10 Oh, that you would bless me and expand my territory.

16:11 Search for the Lord and for his strength; continually seek him.

28:9 For the Lord sees every heart and knows every plan and though.

2 Chronicles 7:14 If my people will humble themselves and pray, I (God) will hear from heaven and will forgive their sins and restore their land.

32:8 We have the Lord our God to help us and to fight our battles for us!

Ezra 3:7 The people begin to rebuild the Temple

3:11 He is so good! His faithful love for Israel endures forever!

4:1 Israel's enemies oppose the rebuilding of the Temple

4:24-5:17 The rebuilding resumes

6:1 King Darius approves the rebuilding of the Temple

Nehemiah 2:18 Yes, let's rebuild the wall! So, they began the good work.

3:1 Rebuilding the Wall of Jerusalem

12:1 The history of the Priests and Levites

12:27 Dedication of Jerusalem's Wall

***Tobit** 2:7 Tobit becomes blind

4:1 Tobit instructs his son Tobiah about the money

5:1 Raphael the Angel is sent by God to help Tobiah on his journey

8:7 Tobiah marries Sarah

9:1 Raphael gets the money from Gabael

13:1 Tobit's praise

13:6 If you turn to Him with all your heart and all your soul to practice truth in his presence, then he will turn to you.

14:6 All the nations of the earth will turn from their ways and will truly worship God.

***Judith** 8:16 Do not try to control the plans of the Lord our God, for God is not like a human being, to be manipulated. He is not like a mere mortal, who can be persuaded.

13:15-16 The Lord has struck him down by the hand of a woman! The Lord protected me in this mission, and as the Lord lives, I swear that it was my beauty that seduced him to his destruction.

***Esther** 4:14 Who knows if perhaps you were made queen for just such a time as this?

3:1-15 Haman's plot against the Jews. He wants to kill all the Jews in the 127 provinces from India to Ethiopia. 7:9 He also built a seventy-five feet tall sharpened pole to impale Mordecai on.   Haman was impaled on his own pole.

8:1 King Xerxes gave the property of Haman's, the enemy of the Jews, to Queen Easter. The Jews were saved from Haman's plot.

8:16 The Jews were filled with joy and gladness and were honored everywhere.

***1 Maccabees 3:19** Success in battle depends not on the size of the Army but on strength that comes from God.

This book talks about the Greek rulers who wanted to conquer the Jews. Time frame was 137th year of Greek rule to the 177th year of Greek rule.

12:15 Our help comes from God.

***2 Maccabees** the battles continue. Very interesting book.

Chapter 7 talks about seven brothers and their mother who were tortured with whips to make them violate the law of Moses by eating pork. They refused to eat the pork and were all killed.

15:21 Battles are not won merely by weapons but according to the Lord's plan.

Job 1:6-12 God allows Satan to test Job.

After Job has lost everything, his animals, farmhands, servants, house and his children, his prayer was - 1:21 The Lord gave me what I had, and the Lord has taken it away. Praise the name of the Lord.

2:11 Job's three friends share in his anguish. They aren't any help.

12:13 True wisdom and power are found in God.

38, 39, 40, and 41 The Lord challenges Job and Job responds to the Lord.

42:12-16 The Lord blessed Job in the second half of his life even more than in the beginning. Job lived 140 years.

Psalms 19:1 The heavens proclaim the glory of God. The skies display his craftsmanship.

23:1-6 The Lord is my shepherd; I have all that I need.

He lets me rest in green meadows; he leads me beside peaceful streams.

He renews my strength.

He guides me along right paths, bringing honor to his name.

Even when I walk through the darkest valley, I will not be afraid, for you are close beside me.

Your rod your staff protect and comfort me.

You prepare a feast for me in the presence of my enemies.

You honor me by anointing my head with oil.

My cup overflows with blessings.

Surely your goodness and unfailing love will pursue me all the days of my life, and I will live in the house of the Lord forever.

27:1 The Lord is my light and my salvation so why should I be afraid?

33:6-9 The Lord merely spoke, and the heavens were created.

He breathed the word, and all the stars were born.

He assigned the sea its boundaries and locked the oceans in vast reservoirs.

Let the whole world fear the Lord, and let everyone stand in awe of him.

For when he spoke, the world began! It appeared at his command.

62:7 My victory and honor come from God alone.

72:1-2 God is honored in Judah; his name is great in Israel.

Jerusalem is where he lives; Mount Zion is his home.

91:2 He alone is my refuge, my place of safety.

97:10 You who love the Lord, hate evil!

118:24 This is the day the Lord has made. We will rejoice and be glad in it.

139:1 O Lord you have examined my heart and know everything about me.

142:5 You are my place of refuge. You are all I really want in life.

150:6 Let everything that breathes sing praises to the Lord!

Proverbs 3:5 Trust in the Lord with all you heart.

6:16-19 & Things God Hates - False witness who lies, haughty eyes, lying tongue, heart that devises wicked schemes, hands that shed innocent blood, person who stirs up conflict in the community and feet that rush into evil.

8:12-14; 9:1 7 Pillars of Wisdom - I know where to discover knowledge and discernment, all who fear the Lord, counsel, insight, power, prudence, and sound judgment.

9:10 Fear of the Lord is the foundation of wisdom. Knowledge of the Holy one results in good judgment.

13:24 Those who spare the rod of discipline hate their children. Those who love their children care enough to discipline them.

16:3 Commit your actions to the Lord, and your plans will succeed.

16:33 We may throw the dice, but the Lord determines how they fall.

17:15 Acquitting the guilty and condemning the innocent, both are detestable to the Lord.

25:24 It's better to live alone in the corner of an attic than with a quarrelsome wife in a lovely home.

28:2 When there is moral rot within a nation, its government topples easily. But wise and knowledgeable leaders bring stability.

28:12 When the godly succeed, everyone is glad. When the wicked take charge, people go into hiding.

31:10-31 The character traits of a virtuous and capable wife.

Ecclesiastes 3:1-8 For everything there is a season,

a time for every activity under heaven.

A time to be born and a time to die. A time to plant and a time to harvest.

A time to kill and a time to heal. A time to tear down and a time to build up.

A time to cry and a time to laugh. A time to grieve and a time to dance.

A time to scatter stones and a time to gather stones.

A time to embrace and a time to turn away.

A time to search and a time to quit searching.

A time to keep and a time to throw away.

A time to tear and a time to mend. A time to be quiet and a time to speak.

A time to love and a time to hate. A time for war and a time for peace.

3:11 God has made everything beautiful for its own time. He has planted eternity in the human heart.

4:9 Two people are better off than one, for they can help each other succeed.

7:13 Accept the way God does things.

8:11 When a crime is not punished quickly, people free it is safe to do wrong.

10:15 Fools are so exhausted by a little work that they can't even find their way home.

10:18 Laziness leads to a sagging roof; idleness leads to a leaky house.

12:1 Honor Him in your youth.

12:13 Fear God and obey His commands, for this is everyone's duty.

12:14 God will judge us for everything we do, including every secret thing, whether good or bad.

Song of Songs 8:7 Many waters cannot quench love, nor can rivers drown it.

***Wisdom** 1: 3 Dishonest thinking separates people from God.

1:4 Wisdom will not enter an evil person, nor will it dwell in a person enslaved by sin.

3:9 Those who trust in the Lord will understand truth, and the faithful will live with him in love. For he shows grace and mercy to his chosen ones.

6:17 The beginning of wisdom is a sincere desire for instruction, and concern for instruction shows a love of wisdom.

8:21 But I knew I could not possess wisdom unless God gave her to me. It was a sign of intelligence that I knew who had given me wisdom.

11:13 For when the ungodly heard that their punishment benefited the righteous, they recognized that the Lord had caused these things to happen.

11:24 For you (God) love everything that exists. You hate none of the things you have made, for you would not have made anything you hated.

***Sirach** (Ecclesiasticus) 1:19 Knowledge and discernment shower down from wisdom.

1:20 Fear of the Lord is the root of wisdom, and long-life stems from her.

3:24 For many have been deceived by their own reasoning, and false assumptions have impaired their judgment.

4:28 Fight for truth even to the point of death, and the Lord God will fight for you.

5:11 Be quick to hear and slow to answer.

6:15 Faithful friends are priceless; their worth can't be measured.

7:1 Do no evil, and no evil will happen to you; avoid wickedness, and it will stay away from you.

8:13 Don't give a guarantee beyond your means; and if you put up bond money for someone, presume you will have to pay it.

11:8 Listen before you answer, and don't interrupt others while they are talking.

11:34 If you receive strangers into your home; they will cause trouble and make you a stranger in your own home.

12:7 Give to the good, but don't help the sinner.

14:15 When you die others will receive your hard-earned possessions, everything you worked for will be randomly distributed to others.

15:19 The Lord watches over those who fear him, and he knows everything we do.

19:2 Wine and women corrupt intelligent men.

20:9 Sometimes hard times can bring good fortune, while a windfall may turn into a loss.

20:18 A slip on the pavement is better than a slip of the tongue.

21:11 The fear of the Lord results in wisdom.

21:15 When intelligent people hear a wise saying, they applaud it and add to it. When fools hear it, they sneer at it and throw it away.

21:26 Fools blurt out whatever they are thinking, but the wise think before they speak.

27:16 Whoever betrays secrets destroys trust and will never find a close friend.

28:1 Those who seek revenge will experience vengeance from the Lord.

28:8 Refrain from quarreling, and you will sin less, for a hot-tempered person provokes arguments.

29:2 Lend to your neighbors in their time of need, and pay your neighbor when your loan is due.

29:23 Be content with little or plenty.

33:2 The wise do not hate the law.

33:14 Good is the opposite of evil, and life is the opposite of death. In the same way, sinners are the opposite of the godly.

36:19 The intelligent mind discerns lies.

39:2 He is careful to remember the sayings of the famous, and he can perceive the subtle truths of parables.

39:33 All the works of the Lord are good, and he will fully supply every need in due time.

Isaiah 1:18 Though your sins are like scarlet, I will make them as white as snow.

2:22 Don't put your trust in mere humans. They are as frail as breath.

3:11 But the wicked are doomed, for they will get exactly what they deserve.

9:6 And He will be called: Wonderful, Counselor, Might God, Everlasting Father, Prince of Peace.

11:6-8 In that day the wolf and the lamb will live together; the leopard will lie down with the baby goat. The calf and the yearling will be safe with the lion, and a little child will lead them all. The cow will graze near the bear. The cub and the calf will lie down together. The lion will eat hay like a cow. The baby will play safely near the hole of a cobra. Yes, a little child will put its hand in a nest of deadly snakes without harm.

24:5-6 The earth suffers for the sins of its people. for they have twisted God's instructions, violated his laws, and broken his everlasting covenant. Therefore, a curse consumes the earth. Its people must pay the price for their sin. The are destroyed by fire, and only a few are left alive.

27:11 Israel is a foolish and stupid nation, for its people have turned away from God.

29:21 Those who convict the innocent by their false testimony will disappear. A similar fate awaits those who use trickery to pervert justice and who tell likes to destroy the innocent.

41:10 Who but a fool would make his own god- an idol that cannot help him one bit.

43:1 I have called you by name; you are mine.

45:19 I would not have told the people of Israel to seek me if I could not be found.

46:13 I am ready to save Jerusalem and show my glory to Israel.

49:8-26 Promises of Israel's Restoration

53:1-12 All about Jesus life and how he died for our sins.

54:14-15 Your enemies will stay far away. You will live in peace and terror will not come near. If any nation comes to fight you, it is not because I sent them. Whoever attacks you will go down in defeat.

60:4 Look and see, for everyone is coming home! Your sons are coming from distant lands, you little daughters will be carried home.

64:8 We are the clay, and you are the potter.

66:16 The Lord will punish the world by fire and by his sword.

Jeremiah 4:3 The coming judgment against Judah

4:23 Jeremiah's Vision of Coming Disaster

5:1 If you can find even on just and honest person, I will not destroy the city.

5: 20 A warning for God's people.

6:16 Judah rejects the Lord's way.   Travel its path, and you will find rest for your souls.

10:1 Idolatry bring destruction.

11:1 Judah's broken covenant.

11:4 If you obey me, I will be your God.

15:1 Judah's inevitable doom.

21:1 No deliverance from Babylon

21:11 Judgment on Judah's Kings

25:1 Seventy years of captivity

29:11 I know the plans I have for you, says the Lord. Plans for good and not for disaster, to give you a future and a hope.

31: 3 I have loved you, my people, with an everlasting love. With unfailing love, I have drawn you to myself.

31:38 The day is coming, says the Lord, when all Jerusalem will be rebuilt for me.

33:1 Promises of peace and prosperity.

43:1 Jeremiah is taken to Egypt.

50:1 A message about Babylon.

50:4 Hope for Israel and Judah

50:11 Babylon's fall

51:36 The Lord's vengeance on Babylon.

52:12 The temple in Jerusalem is destroyed.

52:31 Hope for Israel's royal line.

Lamentations 1:1 Jerusalem, once so full of people, is now deserted. She who was once great among the nations now sits alone like a widow. Once the queen of all the earth, she is now a slave.

2:1 The Lord in his anger has cast a dark shadow over beautiful Jerusalem.

3:22 The faithful love of the Lord never ends! His mercies never cease.

4:11 But now the anger of the Lord is satisfied.

5:21 Restore us, O Lord, and bring us back to you again! Give us back the joys we once had!

***Baruch 1:1** Baruch and the Jews in Babylon.

1:17 We have sinned before the Lord. We have not obeyed him, nor have we listened to the voice of the Lord our God, nor kept the commandments that the Lord gave us.

3:9 Listen, O Israel, to the commandments of life; pay attention, that you may learn wisdom.

4:1 Wisdom is the book of God's commandments, the law that endures forever. Those who keep her will live; those who forsake her will die.

6:70 Those wooden gods, overlaid with gold and silver, are like a corpse thrown out into the darkness.

Ezekiel 4:1 A sign of the coming siege.

5:1 A sign of the coming judgment.

7:1 A coming of the end.

7:27 I will bring on them the evil they have done to others, and they will receive the punishment they so richly deserve. Then they will know that I am the Lord."

7:14 The desolation of Israel.

11:1 Judgment of Israel's leaders

12:1 A new proverb for Israel

12:23 The time has come for every prophecy to be fulfilled!

13:1 Judgment against false prophets.

13:17 Judgment against false women prophets.

13:18 Do you think you can trap others without bringing destruction on yourselves?

13:19 By lying to my people who love to listen lies, you kill those who should not die, and you promise life to those who should not live.

17:3 A story of two Eagles.

20:1 The rebellion of Israel.

24:15 The death of Ezekiel's wife. Yet you must not show any sorrow at her death. Do not weep; let there be no tears.

27:26 The destruction of Tyre.

29:17 Nebuchadnezzar conquers Egypt

30:4 A sword will come against Egypt, and those who are slaughtered will cover the ground.

30:10-11 By the power of King Nebuchadnezzar of Babylon, I will destroy the hordes of Egypt. He and his armies, the most ruthless of all, will be sent to demolish the land.

32:17 Egypt falls into the Pit.

36:1 Restoration for Israel.

36:5 My jealous anger burns against these nations, especially Edom, because they have shown utter contempt for me by gleefully taking my land for themselves as plunder.

37:1 A valley of dry bones.

37:4 Look! I am going to put breath into you and make you live again! I will put flesh and muscles on you and cover you with skin. I will put breath into you, and you will come to life. Then you will know that I am the Lord.

37:15 Reunion of Israel and Judah

43:1 The Lord's Glory returns

48:35 The Lord is there.

Daniel 1:1 Daniel in Nebuchadnezzar's Court

1:7 Daniel was called Belteshazzar, Hanahiah was called Shadrach, Mishael was called Meshach, Zariah was called Abednego.

2:1 Nebuchadnezzar's Dream

2:24 Daniel interprets the Dream

2:26 Nebuchadnezzar rewards Daniel

3:19 The blazing furnace

4:1 Nebuchadnezzar's dream about a tree

4:19 Daniel explains the dream

6:1 Daniel in the lion's den

6:26 He is the living God, and he will endure forever.

7:1 Daniel's vision of four beasts

14:5 I worship the living God, who created heaven and earth and rules over every living being.

Hosea 2:14 The Lord's love for unfaithful Israel

4:1 The Lord's case against Israel

9:1 Hosea announces Israel's punishment

10:1 The Lord's judgment against Israel

11:1 The Lord's love for Israel

14:4 My love will know no bounds.

Joel 1:1 Mourning over Locust plague

2:13 Return to the Lord, your God, for he is merciful and compassionate, slow to get angry and filled with unfailing love.

3:1 Judgment against enemy nations

3:17 Blessings for God's people

Amos 1:3 The people of Damascus have sinned again and again, and I will not let them go unpunished!

2:4 God's judgment on Judah and Israel

5:14 Do what is good and run from evil so that you may live.

5:18 Warning of coming judgment

9:11 A promise of restoration

Obadiah 15 The day is near when I, the Lord, will judge all godless nations! As you have done to Israel, so it will be done to you.

17 Jerusalem will become a refuge for those who escape; it will be a holy place. And the people of Israel will come back to reclaim their inheritance.

Jonah 1:1 Jonah runs from the Lord

2:1-2 Then Jonah prayed to the Lord his God from inside the fish. He said, "I cried out to the lord in my great trouble, and he answered me. I called to you from the land of the dead, and Lord, you heard me!

3:1 Jonah goes to Nineveh

Micah 3:1 Judgment against Israel's leaders

4:6 Israel's return from exile

6:1 The Lord's case against Israel

6:8 The Lord has told you what is good, and this is what He requires of you; to do what is right, to love mercy, and to walk humbly with your God.

7:1 Misery turned to Hope

7:7 I wait confidently for God to save me, and my God will certainly hear me.

7:14 The Lord's compassion on Israel

Nahum 1:2 The Lord's anger against Nineveh

1:7 The Lord is good, a strong refuge when trouble comes, He is close to those who trust in Him.

2:1 The fall of Nineveh

3:1 The Lord's judgment against Nineveh

Habakkuk 1:2 Habakkuk's complaint

1:5 The Lord's reply

3:1 Habakkuk's prayer

3:19 The Sovereign Lord is my strength! He makes me as surefooted as a deer, able to tread upon the heights.

Zephaniah 1:2 The coming judgment against Judah

2:3 Seek the Lord, all who are humble, and follow his commands.

2:8 The judgment against Moab and Ammon

2:12 The judgment against Ethiopia and Assyria

3:1 Jerusalem's rebellion and redemption

Haggai 1:1 A call to rebuild the Temple

1:12 God's people began to obey Him (God)

2:4 Be strong all you people still left in the land. And now get to work, for I am with you, says the Lord of Heaven's Armies.

2:10 Blessings promised for obedience

Zechariah 1:1 A call to return to the Lord

1:3 Return to me, and I will return to you, says the Lord of Heaven's Armies.

2: 6 The exiles are called home

5:1 A flying scroll

8:1 Promised blessings for Jerusalem

9:1 Judgment against Israel's enemies

10:1 The Lord will restore his people

12:1 The future deliverance for Jerusalem

13:9 I (God) will say, "These are my people", and they will say, "The Lord is our God."

14:1 The Lord will rule the earth

Malachi 1:2 The Lord's love for Israel

1:10 A call to faithfulness

1:11 My name is great among the nations, say the Lord of Heaven's Armies.

4:6 His preaching will turn the hearts of fathers to their children, and the hearts of children to their fathers.

New Testament

Matthew 1:1-17 The fourteen generations from Abraham to David, fourteen from David to the Babylonian exile, and fourteen from the Babylonian exile to the Messiah (Jesus). Joseph's line.

1:23 They will call him Immanuel, which means "God is with us."

5:3-10 The Beatitudes

5:13 You are the salt of the earth.

6:9-13 The Lord's Prayer

6:19 Don't store up treasures here on earth, where moths eat them and rust destroys them, and where thieves break in and steal.

6:34 Don't worry about tomorrow, for tomorrow will bring its own worries. Today's trouble is enough for today.

7:7-8 Keep on asking, and you will receive what you ask for. Keep on seeking, and you will find. Keep on knocking, and the door will be opened to you. For everyone who asks, receives. Everyone who seeks, finds. And to everyone who knocks, the door will be opened.

7:12 The Golden Rule - Do to others whatever you would like them to do to you.

8:1-9:34 Jesus's miracles

10:1 Jesus sends out the Twelve Apostles

10:31 So don't be afraid; you are more valuable to God than a whole flock of sparrows.

13:1-52 Jesus 'parables

14:1-12 The death of John the Baptist

14:22 Jesus walks on water

19:26 With God all things are possible.

21:1 Jesus' triumphant entry into Jerusalem

26:1 The plot to kill Jesus

26:17 The Last Supper

26:69 Peter denies Jesus

27:1-5 Judas hangs himself

27:11 Jesus' trial before Pilate

27:45 The death of Jesus

28:1 Jesus' Resurrection of Jesus

28:6 He isn't here! He is risen from the dead, just as he said would happen.

Mark 1:9 The Baptism and Temptation of Jesus

1:21-3:13-19 Jesus chooses the Twelve Apostles

4:1-41 Jesus' parables

6:30 Jesus' feed five thousand

9:23 Anything is possible if a person believes.

11:15 Jesus clears the Temple

11:23 You can say to the mountain, may you be lifted up and thrown into the sea, and it will happen.

14:10 Judas agrees to betray Jesus

14:12 The Last Supper

15:33 The death of Jesus

16:1 The Resurrection of Jesus

16:15 Go into all the world and preach the good news to everyone.

Luke 1:5 The birth of John the Baptist foretold

2:11 The Savior, yes, the Messiah, the Lord, has been born today in Bethlehem, the city of David.

2:14 Glory to God in highest heaven, and peace on earth to those with whom God is pleased.

3:23 Jesus' genealogy from Jesus to God. Mary's line.

6:12 Jesus chooses the Twelve Apostles

10:30 Parable of the Good Samaritan

14:1-16:31 Jesus Parables

18:1 Always pray and never give up.

22:7 The Last Supper

23:26 The Crucifixion

23:44 The death of Jesus

24:1 The Resurrection of Jesus

24:50 Jesus Ascension

24:51-53 While he was blessing them, he left them and was taken up to heaven. So, they worshiped him and then returned to Jerusalem filled with great joy. And they spent all of their time in the Temple, praising God.

John 1:1-5 In the beginning the Word already existed. The Word was with God, and the Word was God. He existed in the beginning with God. God created everything through Him, and nothing was created except through Him. The Word gave life to everything that was created, and His life brought light to everyone. The Light shines in the darkness, and the darkness can never extinguish it.

1:19 The Testimony of John the Baptist

1:35 The First Disciples

3:16 This is how God loved the world. He gave his one and only son, so that everyone who believes in Him will not perish but have eternal life.

7:1 Jesus and His brothers

8:1 A woman caught in adultery

8:32 You will know the truth, and the truth will set you free.

11:1 The Raising of Lazarus

13:1 Jesus washes His Disciples' feet

14:6 I am the way, the truth, and the life.

18:15-27 Peter's 1st, 2nd, and 3rd denials

18:28 Jesus' trial before Pilate

19:1 Jesus sentenced to death

19:17 The Crucifixion

20:1 The Resurrection of Jesus

Acts   1:6 The Ascension of Jesus

1:8 You will receive power when the Holy Spirit comes upon you, and you will be my witnesses.

1:12 Matthias replaces Judas

2:21 Everyone who calls on the name of the Lord will be saved.

6:8 Stephen is arrested

8:4 Philip preaches in Samaria

9:1 Saul's conversion

12:1 James is killed and Peter is imprisoned

12:6 Peter's miraculous escape from prison

13:4 Paul's first missionary journey

15:11 We believe that we are all saved the same way, by the undeserved grace of the Lord Jesus.

16:1 Paul's second missionary journey

16:16 Paul and Silas in prison

17:28 In Him we live and move and exist.

18:1 Paul meets Priscilla and Aquila in Corinth

19:1 Paul's third missionary journey

20:15 Paul arrives in Jerusalem

20:26 Paul is arrested

28:1 Paul on the Island of Malta

Romans 8:28 God causes everything to work together for the good of those who love God.

3:21 Christ took our punishment

6:1 Well then, should we keep on sinning so that God can show us more and more of his wonderful grace?

7:14 Struggling with sin

7:21 I have discovered this principle of life - that when I want to do what is right, I inevitably do what is wrong.

8:31 If God is for us, who can ever be against us?

12:2 Don't copy the behavior and customs of this world, but let God transform you into a new person.

16:17 Paul's final instructions

1 Corinthians 1:3 May God our Father and the Lord Jesus Christ give you grace and peace.

1:10 Divisions in the Church

6:1 Avoiding lawsuits with Christians

6:12 Avoiding sexual sin

7:1 Instruction on marriage

11:26 Every time you eat this bread and drink this cup, you are announcing the Lord's death until he comes again.

12:8-12, 28 Spiritual gifts - apostleship, distinguishing between spirits, encouraging, evangelism, faith, giving, guiding/leading, healing, helping/serving, interpreting tongues, knowledge, miraculous powers, prophecy, showing mercy, speaking in tongues, teaching, wisdom

12:12 One body with many parts

13:4-7 Love is patient and kind. Love is not jealous or boastful or proud or rude. It does not demand its own way. It is not irritable, and it keeps no record of being wronged. It does not rejoice about injustice but rejoices whenever the truth wins out. Love never gives up, never loses faith, is always hopeful, and endures through every circumstance.

15:1 The resurrection of Christ

15:12 The resurrection of the dead

15:22 Everyone who belongs to Christ will be given new life.

15:35 The resurrection body

16:19 Paul's final greetings

2 Corinthians 1:1 Greetings from Paul

3:17 Wherever the Spirit of the Lord is, there is freedom.

5:1 New bodies

5:7 We live by believing and not by seeing.

5:17 Anyone who belongs to Christ has become a new person. The old life is gone; a new life has begun!

11:1 Paul and the false apostles

12:9 My grace is all you need. My power works best in weakness.

13:1 Paul's final advice

13:11 Paul's final greetings

Galatians 1:1 Greetings from Paul

1:6 There is only one Good News

2:20 It is no longer I who live, but Christ lives in me.

3:26 For you are all children of God through faith in Christ Jesus.

5:1 Christ has truly set us free.

5:16 Living by the Spirit's Power

5:22-23 Fruit of the Spirit - But the Holy Spirit produces this kind of fruit in our lives; Love, Joy, Peace, Patience, Kindness, Goodness, Faithfulness, Gentleness, and Self-control. There is no law against these things.

6:9 So let's not get tired of doing what is good. At just the right time we will reap a harvest of blessings if we don't give up.

6:11 Paul's final advice

Ephesians 1:1 Greetings from Paul

1:15 Paul's prayer for Spiritual Wisdom

3:1 God's mysterious plan revealed

3:14 Paul's prayer for Spiritual growth

4:1 Unity in the Body

5:1 Living in the Light

5: 21 Spirit-guided relationships, wives and husbands

6:10-17 The Whole Armor of God - Put on all of God's armor so that you will be able to stand firm against all strategies of the devil. For we are not fighting against flesh and blood enemies, but against evil rulers and authorities of the unseen world, against mighty powers in this dark world, and against evil spirits in the heavenly places. Therefore, put on every piece of God's armor so you will be able to resist the enemy in the time of evil. Then after the battle you will still be standing firm. Stand your ground, putting on the **belt** of truth and the body armor of God's righteousness. For **shoes**, put on the peace that comes from the Good News so that you will be fully prepared. In addition to all of these, hold up the **shield** of faith to stop the fiery arrows of the devil. Put on salvation as your **helmet** and take the **sword** of the Spirit, which is the word of God.

Philippians 1:1 Greetings from Paul

1:20 Paul's life of Christ

2:12 Shine brightly for Christ

3:1 The priceless value of knowing Christ

3:12 Pressing toward the Goal

4:2 Words of Encouragement

4:4 Always be full of joy in the Lord. I say it again- rejoice!

4:6 Don't worry about anything; instead, pray about everything.

4:13 For I can do everything through Christ, who gives me strength.

4:21 Paul's final greetings

Colossians 1:1 Greetings from Paul

1:15 Christ is Supreme

2:6 Freedom from rules a New Life in Christ

2:7 Let your roots grow down into Him, and let your lives be built on Him.

3:1 Living the New Life

3:23 Work willingly at whatever you do, as though you were working for the Lord rather than for people.

4:1 Paul's final instructions and greetings

1 Thessalonians 1:1 Greetings from Paul

2:17 Timothy's good report about the Church

3:12 May the Lord make your love for one another and for all people grow and overflow.

4:1 Live to please God

5:12 Paul's final advice

5:16-18 Always be joyful. Never stop praying. Be thankful in all circumstances.

5:23 Paul's final greetings

2 Thessalonians 1:1 Greetings from Paul

1:3 Encouragement during persecution

2:1 Events prior to the Lord's Second Coming

3:18 May the grace of our Lord Jesus Christ be with you all.

3:16 Paul's final greetings

1 Timothy 1:1 Greetings from Paul

1:3 Warnings against false teachings

1:17 All honor and glory to God forever and ever! He is the eternal King, the unseen one who never dies; he alone is God.

2:1 Instructions about Worship

3:1 Leaders in the Church

4:1 Warning against false teachers

6:1 Paul's final instructions

6:12 Fight the good fight for the true faith.

2 Timothy 1:1 Greetings from Paul

1:3 Encouragement to be faithful

1:7 God has **not** given us a spirit of fear and timidity, but of power, love, and self-discipline.

3:1 The dangers of the last days

3:16 All scripture is inspired by God and is useful to teach us what is true.

3:19 Paul's final greetings

Titus 1:1 Greetings from Paul

2:1 Promote right teaching

3:1 Do what is good

3:5 He saved us, not because of the righteous things we had done, but because of his mercy.

3:12 Paul's final remarks and greetings

3:15 May God's grace be with you all.

Philemon 1 Greetings from Paul

4 I always thank my God when I pray for you.

23 Paul's final greetings

Hebrew 1:1 Jesus Christ in God's Son

1:5 The Son is greater than the angels

4:1 Promised rest for God's people

5:11 A call to Spiritual growth

6:13 God's promises bring hope

6:19 This hope is a strong and trustworthy anchor for our souls.

7:1 Melchizedek is greater than Abraham

7:15 Jesus is like Melchizedek

9:11 Christ is the perfect sacrifice

10:1 Christ's sacrifice once for all

11:1 Faith shows the reality of what we hope for; it is the evidence of things we cannot see.

12:1 Let us run with endurance the race God has set before us.

12:7-8   As you endure this divine discipline, remember that God is treating you as his own children. Who ever heard of a child who is never disciplined by his father? If God doesn't discipline you as he does all of his children, it means that you are illegitimate and are not really his children at all.

12:14 A call to listen to God

James 1:1 Greetings from James

1:2-3 When troubles of any kind come your way, consider it an opportunity for great joy. For you know that when your faith is tested, your endurance has a chance to grow. So let it grow, for when your endurance is fully developed, you will be perfect and complete, needing nothing.

1:17 Whatever is good and perfect is a gift coming down to us from God our Father who created all the light in the heavens.

1:19 You must all be quick to listen, slow to speak, and slow to get angry.

2:14 Faith without good deeds is dead

3:1 Controlling the tongue

4:1 Drawing close to God

4:8 Come close to God, and God will come close to you.

5:13 The power of prayer

5:16 The earnest prayer of a righteous person has great power.

1 Peter 1:1 Greetings from Peter

1:3 The hope of eternal life

1:13 A call to Holy living

4:1 Living for God

4:12 Suffering for being a Christian

5:7 Give all your worries and cares to God, for he cares about you.

5:12 Peter's final greetings

2 Peter 1:1 Greetings from Peter

1:3 Growing in Faith

1:12 Paying attention to Scripture

2:1 The danger of False teachers

3:1 The day of the Lord is coming

3: 17 Peter's final words

3:18 Grow in the grace and knowledge of our Lord and Savior Jesus Christ.

1 John 1:5 Living in the Light

1:7 A new commandment

2:15 Do not love this world

2:18 Warning about the Antichrists

2:28 Living as Children of God

3:11 Love one another

4:1 Discerning false prophets

4:7 Loving one another

4:19 We love each other because He loved us first.

5:1 Faith in the son of God

2 John 1 Greetings from John, the elder

3 Grace, mercy, and peace, which come from God, will continue to be with us.

4 Live the Truth

12 Conclusion

3 John 1 Greetings from John, the elder

4 I could have no greater joy than to hear that my children are following the truth.

13 Conclusion

Jude 1 Greetings from Jude

3 The danger of false teachers

24 A prayer of praise

25 All glory to him who alone is God, our Savior through Jesus Christ our Lord.

Revelation 1:4 John's greeting to the Seven Churches

1:8 I am the Alpha and the Omega, the beginning and the end, says the Lord God.

2:1 The message to the Church in Ephesus

2:8 The message to the Church is Smyrna

2:12 The message to the Church in Pergamum

2:18 The message to the Church in Thyatira

3:1 The message to the Church in Sardis

3:7 The message to the Church in Philadelphia

3:14 The message to the Church in Laodicea

3:20 I stand at the door and knock. If you hear my voice and open the door, I will come in.

4:1 Worship in Heaven

4:8 Holy is the Lord God, the Almighty, the one who always was, who is, and who is still to come.

5:1 The lamb opens the Scroll

6:1 The lamb breaks the First Six Seals

7:1 God's people will be preserved

7:4 And I heard how many were marked with the seal of God, 144,000 were sealed from all the tribes of Israel. Judah, Reuben, Gad, Asher, Naphtali, Manasseh, Simeon, Levi, Issachar, Zebulun, Joseph, Benjamin- each tribe had 12,000, times 12 equals 144,000 each with a seal of God.

8:1 The lamb breaks the Seventh Seal

9:1 The Fifth Trumpet brings the First Terror

10:1 The angel and the Small Scroll

11:1 The Two Witnesses

12:1 The Woman and the Dragon

13:1 The Beast out of the Sea

14:1 The Lamb and the 144,000

15:1 The Song of Moses and of the Lamb

16:1 A mighty voice from the Temple

17:1 The great Prostitute

18:1 The Fall of Babylon

19:1 Songs of Victory in Heaven

20:1 The thousand years

21:1 The New Jerusalem

22:1 A river with the water of life

22:12   I (Jesus) am coming soon.

22:21 May the grace of the Lord Jesus be with God's holy people.

Note from Author

I grew up without computers and cell phones. My family didn't have a TV until I was in the third grade and it had only three channels. We went outside to play and explore the neighborhood with our friends.

Things seem so different today. Students have computers to explain and inform them on what to think. We used sayings to learn by figuring out what they meant. For instance, the quote, "There's more than one way to skin a cat" doesn't literally mean you are going to skin a cat. It means that there is more than one way to do something.

This book of sayings is my way of giving back to others. I can't choose how you learn. I can make this book available for those who have ears to hear and eyes to see. I hope that it will open your minds to a new way of learning. We use these sayings, expressions and pearls of wisdom daily, without being aware of it.

About the Author

I was born Jacqueline Kay Hutchinson, in Winter Haven, Florida, on December 27, 1944. My father was in the Army Air Corps. He grew up in Sumter, South Carolina. My mother was from Scribner, Nebraska. They met during WWII. I had two sisters, Ann and Judy. We ended up in West Palm Beach, Florida, because my dad was in the Air Force stationed at Morrison Field. Today it is Palm Beach International Airport. That is where Presidents John Kennedy and Donald Trump fly into.

I graduated from Forest Hill High School in 1963. We moved back to South Carolina after I graduated from high school. I joined the USMC from 1964 to 1966. I was married to a Marine in November 1965. I had three sons. Teddy in 1966, David in 1967 and Robbie in 1969.

We separated in 1971 and I moved to Charleston, South Carolina, from Cherry Point, North Carolina. I joined the Army Reserves in 1973 and retired in 1993. I was called up for active duty in January 1991 for Desert Storm, and served until January 1992. I was stationed at Fort Dix, New Jersey, and then Fort Jackson, South Carolina. I retired from the Charleston Naval Shipyard in 1994. I also served in the South Carolina State Guard from 2003-2023, a volunteer military organization that responds to disasters and aids communities to recover alongside the National Guard.

I moved to Sumter, South Carolina, in 1998 to help with my mother who had a stroke in February 1998. I have lived here until today. I have been a substitute teacher in Charleston, Dorchester and Sumter Counties. I play the saxophone in church and our community band. I belong to the American Legion and the Marine Corps League 1202. I enjoy politics and attend County Council Meetings. I have traveled to all 50 states and about 18 foreign countries. I lived in Romania for three months. I enjoy genealogy and working in my yard. I enjoyed the time I have spent compiling this book and hope that you will enjoy reading and studying it.

www.ingramcontent.com/pod-product-compliance
Lightning Source LLC
Chambersburg PA
CBHW051208160726
47994CB00002B/514